BRITISH RAILWAYS ILLUSTRATED

Summer Special Number 12

Welcome to British Railways Illustra

ILUSTRATED

Summer Special No.12

Here Comes Summer...

A Midsummer Twelfth Night's Dream in fact... All New Photographs and Articles!

Cover. 60029 WOODCOCK with 'The Capitals Limited' climbing Holloway Bank with the down train in June 1950. Photograph J.C. Flemons, The Transport Treasury.

Frontispiece. Here comes summer (School is out oh happy days) or so the song goes: 5024 CAREW CASTLE heads west with the 9.10am Manchester to Paignton on 6 August 1955. Photograph W. Hermiston, The Transport Treasury.

Rear cover. Camden's 46256 SIR WILLIAM A. STANIER F.R.S. bursts out of Kensal Green tunnel with a down train. Photograph The Transport Treasury.

You'll Remember those Black and White Days...

IRWELL PRESS CO.UK E-mail George@Irwellpress.co.uk

EDITORIAL MATTERS
Contributions, submissions, photographs or whatever (remember the contributor must address and attend to copyright), readers' letters, bouquets and brickbats for British Railways Illustrated must be addressed to Editor,

Chris Hawkins
at 59A, High Street, Clophill, Bedfordshire MK45 4BE
E-mail chris@irwellpress.co.uk
Tel.01525 861888 or
Fax. 01525 862044
Printed & Bound by Newton Printing, London
Copyright :- Irwell Press Ltd. 2004

IRWELL PRESS
No.1 in Railway Publishing

A Rugby Saturday, 21 March 1
Notes By Allan C. Baker

The first of a number of views at the north end of Rugby station, taken from the long footbridge that spanned the tracks just north of Rugby No.5 signal box. Its purpose was to afford pedestrian access to the British Thompson Houston (BTH) Works but it inevitably formed a favourite vantage point for spotters and photographers alike. This is looking over the north side of the bridge (Rugby station lies to the right). On Saturday 21 March 1959 Class 5 44834 of Crewe South has arrived on a Class D partially fitted freight – note head lamp code; one over right buffer and one on top of smoke box. Behind is 8F 48623 of Nuneaton, involved in some sort of shunting move – the wagon in view appears to be an iron ore tippler. Photograph David Horne, The Transport Treasury.

Turning to the south, the view from the BTH bridge took in the north end of Rugby station and all its marvellous trackwork, signals and structures. Carlisle Upperby's 46237 CITY OF BRISTOL has charge of a down express; it is not quite clear which working is involved but it is probably the Euston-Perth, due away from Euston at 1.25pm and from a Rugby stop at 3.0pm. This train also carried through coaches to Blackpool which were detached at Crewe, hence the Restaurant car in the front half of the train – the Blackpool coaches were attached at the rear. The sketchy details available with the original print suggest the train is the Mid-Day Scot but the named trains always had additional carriage roof name boards with the train name on them, and The Mid-Day Scot was a Crewe North diagram at this time. The signal box is Rugby No.5, the LNW usually numbering its signal boxes rather than give them other designations, and the engine would be working through from Euston to Carlisle, hence my view it the Perth, and not the Glasgow train. The Mid-Day Scot changed engines at Crewe, with 5A engines on both legs and in both directions. Almost everything to be seen here has long since disappeared – more's the pity! Photograph David Horne, The Transport Treasury.

Below. A completely different type of train, the 2.40pm Rugby-Leamington Spa (Milverton) 'push-pull' due there at 3.13pm. This is a way of operating, and indeed a connecting line, long since passed into history – in fact the service ceased to run not long after this picture was taken, on commencement of the summer service on 15 June 1959. It fell victim to the continuing process of branch line closures that predated the 'Beeching' era. Four 'push-pull' fitted Ivatt 2-6-2Ts for this service were based on Warwick shed – 41227, 41228, 41285 and 41321. Notice the vacuum operated regulator equipment on the sides of the smoke box and the twin vacuum pipes on the buffer beam on 41228. Photograph David Horne, The Transport Treasury.

A dirty Rugby Class 5, 44863, leaving for the north on the Birmingham line with a light load. The engine has express train head lamps and the 'W' of the reporting number on the head board indicates a special working to a destination on the former Western Division of the London Midland Region. As Rugby too, was on the old Western Division, it does not help us very much! We know the train is heading for the Birmingham route however, from the line it is running on; the line along the Trent Valley is the one to the train's left. Photograph David Horne, The Transport Treasury.

Below. We are now looking north from the bridge again, at what would appear to be the 'north end' pilots. In the foreground is one of those awful (I say this from personal experience of trying to maintain them) North British

330hp 0-4-0 diesel hydraulic shunters, D2910, of which Rugby had a few from new. Some later migrated to Crewe, hence my involvement with them. A fuel tank alongside would be more appropriate than that water column! Behind is one of the early LMS design 'twin motor' diesel electric shunters, 12048. These later became Class 11 and were not fitted with the vacuum brake. The driver standing by it was perhaps in charge of D2910, and trying to arrange a swap! Notice the new 'Rootes Group' cars (Hillman and Singers etc) on the flat wagons, presumably having been brought from Coventry and awaiting onward movement – long before the days of purpose built vehicles for transporting cars. Behind them is the line to Leicester, with part of the BTH works in the background. Photograph David Horne, The Transport Treasury.

You'll Remember those Black and White Days...

Willesden Class 5 45375 makes a spirited start from a Rugby stop – this could be the 12.20pm Saturdays-only Euston to Birmingham via Northampton, due away from Rugby at 3.20pm and into Birmingham at 4.09pm. Once again it can be identified as destined for the Birmingham line, from the route taken. The Class 5 on the van train to the left is 44834, seen in the first view, by this time continuing on its journey south. Photograph David Horne, The Transport Treasury.

This next train is something of a mystery but I reckon it could be the Saturdays-only 12.22pm Watford Junction to Crewe via Northampton. This was due away from its Rugby stop at 2.21pm and into Crewe at 4.4pm; the engine is a nice clean Jubilee, 45584 NORTH WEST FRONTIER of Blackpool, doubtless making its way home after an unbalanced working south. Notice the Western Region coach second from the engine – I wonder how that came about! The main buildings of the BTH factory are very prominent to the extreme left. Photograph David Horne, The Transport Treasury.

Again there is some confusion as to the working shown here. The photographer had an idea that it might be the down Euston-Liverpool Red Rose which did not stop at Rugby and would have been due away from Euston at 12.20pm. It was due into Liverpool Lime Street at 4.8pm and would pass Rugby at around 1.50pm. However, I reckon this is the Mid-Day Scot, always a heavily loaded train and with its diagrammed Crewe North Pacific – so the time would be a little after 2.48pm. The engine is 46225 DUCHESS of GLOUCESTER and if it was a Liverpool train it would almost (without doubt) have been hauled by an Edge Hill Princess Royal Pacific at this time, or perhaps a Royal Scot – Edge Hill did not then have any Duchesses on its books. Photograph David Horne, The Transport Treasury.

Baby Scot 45516 THE BEDFORDSHIRE & HERTFORDSHIRE REGIMENT, drifting into Rugby from the north having, by the look of it, taken rather too much water on Newbold water troughs – note the water spray on the first coach. This was an Edge Hill engine at the time, but that shed would not usually use such an engine on its London turns – and no more were the trains made up of former LMS coaches as this one is. So my guess is that this is the 11.35am Liverpool Lime Street to Rugby, where it was due at 3.24pm. Why the driver chose to take water at Newbold if the train was terminating at Rugby anyway, is lost in the mists of that water spray! Notice all those cars again! Photograph David Horne, The Transport Treasury.

Another long-gone branch line served from the north end of Rugby was that to Leicester, and here we see a Craven three car DMU arriving – note the oil tail lamp still required by the Rule Book, and of course no driver in this, the rear cab. Also worthy of note is the early two-position route indication, and the lack of a yellow warning panel. Once again Rugby No.5 signal box is prominent and there is much to be seen that has long since been swept away. The Leicester route had a rather sparse service and I reckon this train is either the 1.41 or the 3.23pm arrival from Leicester – it was exactly twenty miles and the journey time 46 minutes with five stops. Passenger train services were withdrawn from this route on and from 1 January 1962 – one of the early closures of the 'Beeching' era. Photograph David Horne, The Transport Treasury.

Next in this selection we have one of the afternoon Manchester-London trains approaching Rugby, passing the No.5 signal box in the charge of Jubilee 45686 ST VINCENT, a Camden engine at the time. Once again the actual train details are not given, but by my reckoning it is the 12 noon from Manchester London Road, which was not booked to stop at Rugby (pass at 2.10pm) and was non-stop from Stoke-on-Trent to Euston, where it was due at 3.56pm. This had been for many years a Camden diagram, while the later train, the 2pm from London Road which also ran via Stoke-on-Trent, was a Longsight job and almost always a 9A Britannia Pacific. The tender still sports the earlier 'cycling lion' emblem; to the left is the BTH factory, later part of the AEI, and later still the GEC empire. Photograph David Horne, The Transport Treasury.

This is described as a Wolverhampton-Euston train; it is certainly on the line coming from the direction of Birmingham and I'd wager it is the 1.48pm Wolverhampton to Euston, due away from Rugby at 3.18pm and into Euston 4.44pm. The train engine is Bushbury Jubilee 45742 CONNAUGHT and the pilot a dirty and unidentified Class 5. This would almost certainly be an unbalanced engine working home to either Camden or Willesden, as at this time these trains were the sole preserve of the Bushbury Jubilees. Photograph David Horne, The Transport Treasury.

Below. A change of scene, to the north, on the Trent Valley line, though some deduction is required! Crewe North's 46251 CITY OF NOTTINGHAM got this early version of the maroon livery with BR-style lining (as did a few others) in November 1958, before LMS-style lining became standard. An Up train, it might just be The Royal Scot,

non-stop Carlisle-Euston. Due away from Carlisle at 11.57am, it would pass Rugby a little after 4pm to reach Euston at 5.30pm; notice there is no coal showing in the tender, indicating a lengthy working. The Royal Scot at this time was diagrammed for Camden and Carlisle engines on alternate days, so we have to muse on how a 5A machine came to be in charge; if indeed it *is* The Royal Scot! But if my ideas on the time of day are correct, this would be the only train in this direction diagrammed for a Pacific. The day time Perth-Euston, which *would* have a Crewe North Pacific, was not due at Rugby until 5.54pm, by which time the sun would be lower, and I reckon our photographer would have gone home! Notice the fireman 'playing' with the exhaust injector, which is losing water, doubtless having 'knocked off' (it should not have done if adjusted properly) when the driver shut off to coast through the station. Photograph David Horne, The Transport Treasury.

You'll Remember those Black and White Days...

Riley's Railway Roundabout

The Cross, 16 September 1961 Notes by Eddie Scrumpter

A4 Pacifics 60003 ANDREW K. McCOSH and 60014 SILVER LINK, together with A1 60141 ABBOTSFORD and V2 60800 GREEN ARROW outside the main shed at Kings Cross on 16 September 1961. The grand old place is still in all its glory of course, despite the all-conquering DMUs and the growing threat of main line diesels. This was the last full year of the non-stop Elizabethan and almost an end of term air seemed to prevail. Steam was still everywhere on the GN and, furthermore, was putting in heroic efforts on optimistic diagrams introduced for diesels. As the latter flunked embarrassingly, the Pacifics proved up to the task beyond all expectations. Photographs R.C. Riley, The Transport Treasury.

The 'Met' shed. Surprisingly, it was local passenger work which formed the greater part of Top Shed's duties. The N2s' suburban work had begun to go to DMUs at the end of 1958 and most of the rest followed in 1959. Only five of the N2s remained by early 1962 (such as 69538 here, which was observed working the Flying Scotsman empty stock) but all had gone by May that year. Some L1 2-6-4Ts at this time, such as 67793 and 67749 alongside our sprightly N2, were still available for empty stock working but they too seem to have faded away in 1962. Photographs R.C. Riley, The Transport Treasury.

You'll Remember those Black and White Days...

These four pictures show the progress of **60500 EDWARD THOMPSON** on the shed that day. The turntable was out of action and the A2/3 has already turned after arrival at the station. It has thus come on the shed 'pointing north' rather than the other way round and has coaled before running onto this spur (lockers and cycle shed to right, part of the old semi-circular shed above) to reverse back to the head of the shed yard. The lower picture shows 60500 running forward, past the ash crane. The spur in the first picture, above, actually lies behind the coaling plant in the lower view. Photographs R.C. Riley, The Transport Treasury.

Above, EDWARD THOMPSON is nearly at the head of the yard but has yet to proceed past the turntable (undergoing renewal) and under York Way to reverse back to the shed. Below, there he goes! off to the servicing pits (the 'back pits') laid out by the LNER in the 1930s. Photographs R.C. Riley, The Transport Treasury.

You'll Remember those Black and White Days...

Above, **60060 THE TETRARCH** on shed that day; an NER engine, it visited London more than once during this period. It was far from alone in this, in fact, and other A3s from Newcastle were turning up. This was all doubtless due to the venerable Pacifics finding themselves on the shiny Type 4 diagrams – a Neville Hill A3 could turn up at Kings Cross after hauling a train all the way up from Edinburgh, amid other wonders. Below is one of the last five N2 0-6-2Ts at the Cross, 69593 in poor external nick though still working. Photographs R.C. Riley, The Transport Treasury.

Good old GREEN ARROW again; we were grateful for a named V2 as it pounded underneath 'Skelly Bridge ' at Oakleigh Park but it sometimes seemed too much of a good thing. Where were the others? we wondered, knowing little of the territorial restrictions imposed on the engines of the East Coast. Finally, below, that turntable, under renewal with only some two years left for Top Shed. It is curious but in fact both the turntables, at Top Shed and the station, were replaced, because of age and infirmity. If the engineer responsible had condemned the turntable on a particular date, then that was that. The replacements were redundant 70ft units from the GE and M&GN, which were provided for some reason in the past and were hardly used where they were originally installed. The cost would not have been that outrageous as the replacements were already to hand. Still, a rum do... Photographs R.C. Riley, The Transport Treasury.

You'll Remember those Black and White Days...

Willesden Visit

Two typical scenes at Willesden in the early 1960s. The battle-scarred 3F tank has been involved in some sort of side scrape – the first scarring begins near the side tank front, gradually becoming more severe until the bunker which, judging from the magnitude of the 'chunk' quarried out, was what finally brought the errant movement to an end. These were frequent occurrences, hardly worthy of note – in this instance, no doubt, something was left foul and was not spotted by the crew until it was too late. The impact would certainly have set the coal flying, had it been as artfully stacked up as it is now. Few modellers would dare to replicate the distorted and collapsing coal rails and near-horizontal extension plate. This Jinty is right-hand drive – reversing lever prominent in 'mid-gear'. The Royal Scot at the front of the shed, 46101 ROYAL SCOTS GREY, had been one of the Camden express fleet transferred from Camden on their ousting by diesels in 1961. AWS but no speedo, engine pickers will notice, and a nice dribble of condensed water from the exhaust taps. Photographs The Transport Treasury.

A typical George Heiron night-time shot, at Mangotsfield – a fairly well-known one but deserving of another outing. George liked the idea of the railway almost lost in the landscape and, of course, he wasn't slow in bringing it home to us that this effect was only heightened at night. Photograph G. Heiron, courtesy Mrs Shirley Heiron and The Transport Treasury.

You'll Remember those Black and White Days...

FREEMAN'S FORAYS

T9 4-4-0 in its perambulations at Andover Junction; it would be heading for the Romsey line, where is stayed until it could reverse back to head the 11.25am to Eastleigh. Photograph L.R. Freeman, The Transport Treasury.

Leslie Freeman made many railway trips in the 1950s and 1960s, searching out steam and rejecting diesels, recording his experiences and impressions along the way. A number of these Freeman's Forays *are being published in* British Railways Illustrated *magazine and in our Summer Specials and Annuals. Keep a look out for them!*

Waterloo to Andover Junction, Andover Junction to Swindon, Swindon to Calne and return, Swindon to Kemble, Kemble to Cirencester Town and return; Kemble to Tetbury and return; Kemble to Paddington – Wednesday 21st August 1957.

I travelled from Waterloo to Andover Junction on the 9 o'clock West of England train. On arrival at Waterloo I found this consisted of thirteen corridors, about 430 tons tare, 475 tons gross, headed by Merchant Navy Pacific 35030 ELDER DEMPSTER LINES, in original condition. Standing in an adjacent platform waiting to back out was N15 30738 KING PELLINORE and the empty stock of the 9am had been brought in by M7 0-4-4T 30241.

Departure was to the stroke of nine but bad slipping marred it. Clapham Junction, where H16 4-6-2T 30517 was shunting, was passed in 7½ minutes and there followed some hard work through Earlsfield. Despite this, Surbiton was reached nearly a minute late. At Wimbledon I noted Q1 0-6-0 33017 proceeding down the Mitcham line. We spent a minute and a half in Surbiton but left with only a slight slip and accelerated well. The crew really set to work to recover the lost time, which they were successful in doing. Speed rose to 71mph past West Byfleet and we stopped in Woking rather over a minute early, having run the 12.4 miles from Surbiton in 14 minutes 25 seconds, start to stop. It must be mentioned though that whereas we arrived a shade before 9.35am, some public timetables give the departure as 9.35am, others as 9.36am. Be that as it may, nearly three minutes were occupied in station work, 35030 then got in dead centre, as a result of which our exit was somewhat slippery, and finally we ran into a severe permanent-way slack just after passing Farnborough. As a result of these checks and despite a good climb to MP31 and a 72mph after Hook, Basingstoke (where we were due at 10.4am) was reached 4¾ minutes late.

The crew then took water and so our station allowance of a minute was lengthened to three. Once some initial bad slipping had been overcome, some fine running was made to Andover Junction and two minutes were regained, thus making our arrival at the latter station 4¾ minutes late. Maximum speed on this stretch had been about 75mph through Hurstbourne and generally the run had been quite creditable, particularly as the engine was not in the best of condition. She slipped badly once or twice at speed and the valve gear was a little out of phase.

Observations from Wimbledon were as follows: at Woking, M7 30675 in the north yard and Standard Class 5 73114 on an up goods; near Brookwood, Standard Class 4 4-6-0 75075 on an up train and, at Basingstoke station, G6 30258 shunting and V 30905 TONBRIDGE on a Reading train. On Basingstoke shed were Standard Class 4 75079, H15 30523, Q1 33004 and N15s 30456 SIR GALAHAD, 30748 VIVIEN and 30785 SIR MADOR DE LA PORTE.

You'll Remember those Black and White Days...

Leslie Freeman's train for Swindon arrives at Andover off the Romsey line behind 'U Boat' 31639, hauling three GW coaches. Photograph L.R. Freeman, The Transport Treasury.

At Andover Junction I had a wait of half an hour before my train on to Swindon. Outside the shed were Standard Mogul 76007, U 31803, T9 30117, a second T9 just protruding out of the shed and, a most surprising find, the stove-pipe chimney of Q 30549, a Norwood engine. Another U-boat, 31801, was shunting in the yard and while I waited 2-6-0 6330 arrived with an up goods which it shunted into the yards. T9 30117 also came into action, coming off shed and backing into the carriage sidings, emerging a little later with three South Western coaches which she took down the Romsey line a little way.

Savernake High Level, looking backwards from the northbound train. Apparently the shabby building had once been the Marquess of Ailesbury's private waiting room and originally a footbridge was provided – it stood between the large middle bush and the station building. Photograph L.R. Freeman, The Transport Treasury.

Ogbourne. A modest station to serve a hamlet, its most notable traffic in earlier years had been race horses to and from a private siding to the south. Photograph L.R. Freeman, The Transport Treasury.

There it stayed, waiting for the 10.10am ex-Southampton Terminus to arrive before reversing back into the station to form the 11.25am to Eastleigh. The 10.10am was the train that I was waiting for and it pulled in off the Romsey line a minute late at 11.4am, made up of three Great Western corridor coaches headed by U 31639.

Departure was a minute late at 11.6am. From Andover Junction the MSWJ trains run on a track parallel to the South Western main line for some way to Red Post Junction where the MSWJ doubles and curves away to Weyhill, a station with neat red brick buildings on the up (to Andover) side but only a dilapidated signalbox and flimsy timber shelter on the down. From Weyhill the line continues to Ludgershall, formerly the branch junction for Tidworth. The platforms here are wide and spacious, the down one being graced by a substantial red brick signalbox, iron overbridge, large water tank and a dilapidated wooden shelter. The short bay from which Tidworth trains once ran has had its track lifted. The up platform is an island although probably only the inside face is used. This platform has large, neat red brick offices. Finally, on the far side of the station was another grass covered platform. The Tidworth

branch itself curves away immediately north of Ludgershall through extensive War Department yards.

We did not stop at Collingbourne nor at Collingbourne Kingston Halt where, on more favourable grades, 31639 suddenly awoke from a gentle trot into a good gallop. Grafton and Burbage was passed at speed and then came perhaps the most interesting section of the journey, from Grafton South Junction to Marlborough. First, at the former, the now disused connection down to Grafton East Junction came in; the track was still in position but all signals have been dismantled. Immediately, the lines down to the main line at Savernake (Low Level) diverged, leaving us to follow a single track line to Savernake (High Level). This latter station is in a dilapidated state and the up side platform is disused, the loop being full of wagons. A few people, including some spotters, alighted, the latter making their way to the Low Level station. After leaving Savernake (High Level) away to the west another single line, from Low Level, comes into view and slowly straggles and rises towards the High Level line. Eventually, the two lines meet but do not form a junction, running together as two single tracks for a

considerable way. Passing through a short tunnel, at the exit we encountered a full stop for signals, the lines joining just outside Marlborough station. This station lies on a curve with red brick buildings on the down side and a large corrugated shelter on the up. Two engines were shunting in the quite extensive yards, one a pannier tank and the other a Standard 4, 4-6-0, 75003.

Northwards from Marlborough, the line singles with passing loops at the intermediate stations, Ogbourne and Chiseldon. At the former there is a corrugated shelter on the down platform with the principal buildings on the up side, where 2-6-0 6373 was waiting with the 10.8am ex-Cheltenham Spa. We left together. Chiseldon differs from Ogbourne in having the main station offices on the down side and lies in a shallow cutting. Here we passed 2-6-0 6370 on an up goods. Nearing Swindon Town the line doubles, runs past a fair-sized goods yard and into the station which has three platforms and substantial red brick offices on the up side. The outer face of the down side island platform is used by the connecting train to Swindon Junction. I should emphasis that I have called the Andover Junction direction 'up' only because trains travelling that way face London at Andover.

Leaving Andover the line undulates and curves its way fairly gently across Salisbury Plain. However, after Savernake, the curvature becomes increasingly more severe as the line runs into the Marlborough and Berkshire Downs. The countryside becomes more wooded and picturesque and Ogbourne, in particular, is a very pleasant station. Finally, between Chiseldon and Swindon Town, the line is practically walled in by trees. Then comes Swindon, an unfamiliar side to the town with some quite pleasant suburban streets, the existence of which is completely unsuspected by the traveller on the main line.

I alighted at Swindon Town and watched 31639 take water. The U had arrived two minutes early at 12.17pm, despite a very leisurely run. Little effort had been made on the earlier part of the journey and no speed of any note attained until the line suddenly began to drop near Collingbourne. After that a more sustained effort was made but the schedule certainly does not tax the capabilities of either the Western or

the Southern Moguls. 31639 left on time at 12.25pm and I then joined the two well-filled coaches forming the 12.38pm to Swindon. Motive power was supplied by Penzance! in the shape of pannier 9748, running-in ex-shops of course.

Leaving Swindon Town the line traverses a short tunnel and then curves round a hill on the outskirts of Swindon until Rushey Platt Station signalbox. Here the main line, which singles immediately after leaving Swindon Town, doubles again and passing over the Bristol line continues on past the rear of the Works and under the Swindon to Gloucester line. By that point, however, the line has singled again. Returning to Rushey Platt Station signalbox, a double-track spur leaves the MSWJ and drops down to join the Bristol line at Rushey Platt Junction. Half way down this spur we were held by signals for an up train on the main line and while we stood there 2-8-0 2836, ex-shops, passed by light from Swindon to Swindon Town. After a short wait we were allowed on to the main line and ran past the Works into the station. I noted outside the Works 9722 shunting, 8461, 9600, 5816,

5330 resplendent in lined-green livery, 5724, 9790, 7206, 5710 and 0-6-2T 397 also shunting. At the station itself 0-6-0PT 9476 was on pilot work.

Having re-booked to Calne and been issued with a Great Western Railway ticket which I managed to retain intact, I joined the 1 o'clock all stations to Bristol made up of eight corridors and two vans headed by 5919 WORSLEY HALL. Two down trains went through, 5065 NEWPORT CASTLE on the 11.5am Paddington to Gloucester and 5006 TREGENNA CASTLE and we followed the latter down to Chippenham at 1.1pm. On an easy schedule 5919 ran steadily and with short stops at Wootton Bassett, Dauntsey and Christian Malford Halt arrived at Chippenham punctually at 1.33pm. She pulled up twice there in order to get the vans into the platform. The only engine noted en route was 0-6-0PT 4651 shunting at Wootton Bassett while outside Chippenham shed was 0-6-0PT 3645. 9795 was shunting and 0-4-2T 1433 came out of the yard, after 5919 had departed, pulling two motor coaches. I thought that it was the 1.51pm to Calne but on investigation found it was the

A little further on, at Chiseldon. It was similar to Ogbourne, though the settings were rather different. Photograph L.R. Freeman, The Transport Treasury.

Swindon Town and the notorious bag. Inside lurked the bottle of orange squash that was to lose its cork later in the day – with such a debilitating effect on the morale of our narrator. Photograph L.R. Freeman, The Transport Treasury.

1.50pm to Westbury. The former, I discovered, was 0-6-0PT 8744 and three coaches which had arrived at 1.40pm, the 12.35pm ex-Bristol (Temple Meads). 8744 stood at the platform taking water before drawing out a minute early at 1.50pm with three well-filled coaches.

The single line to Calne curves away to the south immediately on the London side of Chippenham and follows a curving and undulating course, particularly after Stanley Bridge Halt, the two miles course before that halt following fairly flat

The abandoned Rushey Platt station and junction. Photograph L.R. Freeman, The Transport Treasury.

country. Around Black Dog Hill the line runs through wooded country and Black Dog Halt is very picturesquely situated. It is rather more impressive than Stanley Bridge but trains only stop there when requested. There being no-one for the halt on the outward trip, 8744 steamed merrily through it and wended her way into Calne. The terminus has one platform, long enough to accommodate 8744 and her train and a line of vans. The station buildings are undistinguished, some having been added to deal with increased wartime traffic. The latter is still quite heavy, including a good amount for the Royal Air Force and the large yard and the vans in the platform were evidence of the considerable freight traffic. 8744 ran round her train and a standard van was added to the rear. Before leaving I spent a few minutes chatting to the driver who remembered the days when this through working to Bristol was a steam railcar. He took a dim view of using panniers on main line traffic and thought a speed limit should be imposed on them.

We left Calne a couple of minutes late at 2.32pm and ran briskly but uneventfully back to Chippenham, except that somebody alighted at Black Dog Halt. The 2.30pm terminated at Chippenham and 8744 drew her train down the main line as another pannier, 7721, arrived with the 2.16pm ex-Bath Spa. The latter reversed back into the lay-by

siding between the up and down main lines and alongside 8744. They were still shunting when at 2.54pm, a minute early, 5974 WALLSWORTH HALL drew in with the 2.8pm Westbury to Swindon slow. Her load was eight moderately filled corridors and a van. Once again, the main line journey was quiet, punctual and uneventful; the only locomotive of note being 0-4-2T 1462 outside Chippenham shed.

Back at Swindon, I managed to persuade the ticket collector there to allow me to retain the Calne ticket which made me feel a little more cheerful. I then booked to Kemble and obtained some liquid refreshment to replace that lost at Chippenham when the cork came out of the bottle as it lay in my bag. Some railwayman in the yard noticed the trail of orange squash as I walked down the platform and after some vigorous shouting called it to my attention. As a result, part of my time on the Calne branch and on the journey back to Swindon was spent in drying out the contents of my bag, principally my plastic mackintosh. At one time I felt like going home, but decided to press on. By Swindon my spirits had risen considerably and the appearance of my favourite Castle, 5042 WINCHESTER CASTLE on the train to Kemble, completed my recovery. The train was the 2.15pm ex-Paddington; it arrived early, detached its rear portion and then continued its journey (due off 3.52pm) nearly half a minute early.

With a moderate load of seven corridors 5042 made a speedy run to Kemble, reaching 70mph at Oaksey Halt and despite a slowing for considerable permanent-way work before and in Kemble tunnel, the latter station was reached about three minutes early. There I was met by a wonderful sight: two branch trains standing in their respective platforms, both steam hauled. The station itself is of sturdy stone construction and the Tetbury line train occupies a bay at the northern end of the down platform, with a goods siding beside it. The short Cirencester branch platform curves at an angle with the up platform and the branch has a direct junction with the main line so that Cirencester trains can, if necessary, continue through to Swindon. The main station offices are situated in the angle formed by the Cirencester and up platforms, and there are 2 further goods roads beside the Cirencester platform and more to the north of the station where the aspect is dominated by a large signalbox and an even larger water tank; to the south is Kemble tunnel.

With the Tetbury branch train not due to leave until 5.10pm, I first travelled to Cirencester Town. Both branches are similar in that they curve sharply away from the main line on leaving Kemble and both run through some lovely countryside. The Cirencester line, however, is much shorter and until approaching its terminus follows a gentle course.

Re-booking to Calne at Swindon and clutching the unexpected prize of a GWR ticket, Leslie Freeman awaited his train to Chippenham behind 5919 WORSLEY HALL. In the meantime, 5065 NEWPORT CASTLE left with the 11.5am Paddington-Gloucester. Photograph L.R. Freeman, The Transport Treasury.

You'll Remember those Black and White Days...

Typical GWR 'pagoda' corrugated shelter at Stanley Bridge Halt on the Calne branch. Viewed from the train of 'three well-filled coaches' hauled by pannier 8744. Photograph L.R. Freeman, The Transport Treasury.

Near Cirencester it follows round the base of a hill in a curve of about 90 degrees, then runs into the terminus past a large yard and a small shed, which still appears in use. The track was in excellent condition and I gather that the branch recently boasted the best length in the Bristol division. The station itself has one platform and imposing white-washed buildings and, wonder of wonders for a branch terminus, is being modernised. Presumably, this is one branch that is not threatened with closure; certainly the train in both directions was well-filled when I travelled. Motive power appears to be provided by pannier tanks from Swindon with two coach trains. I travelled on the 4.25pm from Kemble which was hauled by 3763. The latter made a smart run, ran round its train and returned from Cirencester at 4.47pm. Actually, a late passenger resulted in the train being brought to a sudden stop just as we were starting off. Nevertheless, Kemble was reached punctually at 4.55pm. There 3763 took water and later continued on to Swindon as the 5.15pm, the branch train being taken over by 9772 which had arrived at Kemble with the branch freight just before we departed at 4.25pm. At the back of the freight train was attached the spare branch coach set with which 9772 formed the 5.8pm to Cirencester. While the

changeover was taking place, 5065 NEWPORT CASTLE arrived three minutes late with the 3.55pm Cheltenham Spa to Paddington, due Kemble 5pm, and 0-6-2T 6699 was shunting goods wagons in the down yard alongside the Tetbury branch train. This latter consisted of 0-4-2T 5804 and a single coach.

An immediate contrast with the Cirencester line was the grassy branch bay, while from the platform it was clear the track was badly overgrown on the branch itself. The latter immediately curves away very sharply and starts climbing at 1 in 60, a by no means pleasant start for a loaded goods train on a wet day with probably nothing more than an 0-4-2T and so the line continues right up to Tetbury. There is now only one intermediate stopping place, Rodmarton Platform, a timber platform with a corrugated shelter. Another halt between there and Kemble built during the Second World War to serve a nearby airfield has now completely disappeared except for two iron supports. A short distance further on from Rodmarton is, or was, the branch's main intermediate station, Culkerton. The single platform has substantial brick buildings with a goods siding and a large timber mill or warehouse; all is now completely derelict, the station is closed, the rails are red with rust and overgrown. Even the sleepers on the branch line are

completely covered by a carpet of green and except for the two shining rails running past the platform, one coming upon the spot casually would at once assume that the whole was part of yet another abandoned railway. The rest of the branch is also badly overgrown although not quite so much as at Culkerton.

Tetbury terminus is a neat brick building with a rather short platform and a run round loop which drives into the hillside. Before the station is a sizeable goods yard and a small shed in which the engine is still stabled overnight. Passenger traffic appeared moderate but unfortunately the line is duplicated by a road for much of the way. Freight varies but in the past has been heavy. According to the driver the fate of the line is still uncertain but he was sceptical about the early arrival of a railcar, forecast in 'The Railway Observer' recently.

Naturally speeds on the branch were restrained; I travelled on the 5.10pm which had a fair number of passengers, all for Tetbury, Rodmarton being passed without stopping, a usual procedure I found out later. The guard ascertains whether anybody wants to alight there before the train leaves Kemble or Tetbury and then if nobody is on the platform the driver continues on. I had rather over half an hour at Tetbury which I passed pleasantly enough in photographing the

A somnolent Calne terminus. Photograph L.R. Freeman, The Transport Treasury.

charming, peaceful station and in chatting to the fireman, a relief from Gloucester who had just taken over from the regular man. I think he thought the branch a little too quiet; he was a young fellow just out of the Army and mentioned an unfortunate experience at Lydney with one of the new 'Inter City' express diesel trains running between Birmingham and South Wales – it broke down at the aforesaid station and they had to wait for a steam train to come up from Gloucester.

The train awaits return from Calne to Chippenham. Photograph L.R. Freeman, The Transport Treasury.

8744 ready to leave Calne – on the left is the driver who took such a dim view of using pannier tanks on the main line. Photograph L.R. Freeman, The Transport Treasury.

The fireman did not know what had happened to the driver who had apparently said he was going home for tea and promptly disappeared. However, the driver arrived back and to my great delight invited me to ride back on the footplate. Once again, Rodmarton was passed without stopping but we called at Culkerton and I was able to obtain a photograph. The journey was uneventful; speeds, of course, were not high and despite the overgrown track, the 0-4-2T rode well bunker first. The driver had been on the branch since February, replacing a gentleman who had been there for thirty years. This latter character was presumably the relation of a railway enthusiast friend who spent most of his time trying to find a locomotive which could surmount the 1 in 60 out of Kemble with a heavy goods. He came nearest to achieving this ambition when he got hold of a 57XX pannier tank. Although, officially, banned from the branch, he cheerfully used it for sometime having at last an engine which was the master of the branch. Alas, one evening approaching Tetbury the coach and some wagons came off the rails and investigation by high authorities located the trouble as spreading of the track caused by the 57XX. So the driver had perforce to return to his 14XX, 58XX, 16XX and 74XX engines. He

did, however, have one further attempt at getting something better. One day a 94XX pannier tank appeared at Kemble and he was almost off up the branch with it when the signalman spotted the red restriction disc and refused to let him go!

I came back from Tetbury on the 6.5pm which connected with two possible trains back to Swindon, both of which connected at Swindon with the train back to Paddington. The first of these, the 5.38pm Cheltenham to Swindon semi-fast arrived three minutes late at 6.52pm behind 4-6-0 6822 MANTON GRANGE. I let this train go and caught the second, the 7 o'clock all stations Kemble to Swindon which consisted of four coaches headed by 0-6-0PT 4651. The train had been standing in the sidings to the north of the station and very quickly followed 6822 into the platform. We departed on time and 4651 put on an extremely vigorous and fast performance, which provided an interesting contrast to the opinion of the driver at Calne earlier in the day as to the suitability of these engines for main line work. This specimen must have obtained all of 50mph between stations and despite a full stop for signals near the junction, arrived at Swindon two minutes early at 7.29pm. Passing the shed I noticed standing outside

rebuilt Merchant Navy 35025 BROCKLEBANK LINE her testing plant trials evidently completed.

I then returned to Paddington on the 4.35pm ex-Taunton, due at Swindon at 7.41pm. In the short intervening time I observed an immaculate Britannia, 70019 LIGHTNING, arrive and depart on the down 'Red Dragon', running about five minutes late, while in the yards were 4-6-0s 5918 WALTON HALL ex-shops and 6960 RAVENINGHAM HALL, 2-8-0 2809 and 0-6-0PTs 5737 and 7792. The 4.35pm arrived five minutes early at 7.36pm with 7034 INCE CASTLE at the head of seven corridors. We waited until 7.45pm and then 7034 made a fast run to Didcot, arriving four minutes early at 8.10pm. 72mph was attained at Wantage Road. We stayed 8½ minutes at Didcot, during which time WD 2-8-0 90125 went through on an up goods. However, the chief sight, and one that attracted considerable attention even among the passengers, was 3440 CITY OF TRURO, which had just previously worked in on the 4.56pm ex-Southampton Terminus and was busy stowing her train away.

We left Didcot half a minute late but easily recovered this with a 77mph through Pangbourne. Signals between Tilehurst and Reading delayed our final progress but,

Back at Swindon – this is Leslie Freeman's favourite, 5042 WINCHESTER CASTLE with the train that would take him to Kemble, the 2.15pm ex-Paddington. Photograph L.R. Freeman, The Transport Treasury.

nevertheless, we drew to a stand at Reading exactly on time at 8.39pm. We were due to depart at 8.45pm but at that precise time we were overtaken on the up fast through road by the 'South Wales Pullman' running very late. We departed on its tail a minute and a half late but, alas, its progress continued to be somewhat lethargic. Checks as a result of it were encountered at Slough, West Drayton and Southall

The 4.25pm Cirencester train at Kemble, a Swindon 57XX pannier tank, 3763 with two coaches. Photograph L.R. Freeman, The Transport Treasury.

You'll Remember those Black and White Days...

3763 after arrival at Cirencester and running round, ready to depart back to Kemble as the 4.47pm. Just as it started off, it came to an abrupt halt to allow a late passenger on the train! Photograph L.R. Freeman, The Transport Treasury.

and culminated in dead stands at Acton and Ranelagh Bridge and a six minute late arrival at Paddington at 9.31pm, a most unfortunate end to a fine journey and, indeed, an excellent day. One final note on the engines noted at Reading. These were 0-6-0PT 4661, 2-6-0s 6302 and 9309, Standard 2-6-0 76017 on the 8.38pm to Basingstoke, Standard 5 73012 on a down empty stock train composed of LMS stock, 0-4-2T 1436 in the centre bay and 4-6-0 7014 CAERHAYS CASTLE on the 8.5pm Paddington to Bristol.

The branch train after arrival back at Kemble. After taking water it went forward to Swindon as the 5.15pm, while the branch train was taken over by 9772. Photograph L.R. Freeman, The Transport Treasury.

You'll Remember those Black and White Days...

The Tetbury bay at the west side of Kemble. The Tetbury branch train waits, 0-4-2T 5804 and a single coach. The 0-6-2T 6699 was shunting goods wagons in the down yard alongside. Photograph L.R. Freeman, The Transport Treasury.

After arrival at the little Tetbury terminus, 5804 moves forward to its run round loop which 'drove into the hillside' as Freeman so aptly put it. Photograph L.R. Freeman, The Transport Treasury.

You'll Remember those Black and White Days...

And pauses alongside the diminutive engine shed. Photograph L.R. Freeman, The Transport Treasury.

The prospect towards Kemble, Tetbury engine shed to right and the substantial goods shed in front. Two lengthy sidings curved round to the right for some distance, alongside the course of the branch. Photograph L.R. Freeman, The Transport Treasury.

Leslie Freeman, prowling the pleasantly sleepy area of the little terminus, take a last portrait of the station. Photograph L.R. Freeman, The Transport Treasury.

5804 'ready and rounded' and now heading bunker first for Kemble. Photograph L.R. Freeman, The Transport Treasury.

You'll Remember those Black and White Days...

Top left. On this latest Foray we are back at Kemble now, after the return from Tetbury. Since 3763's departure for Swindon, 9772 has been looking after the Cirencester branch workings. Photograph L.R. Freeman, The Transport Treasury.

Below left. In between workings, 9772 shunts a horse box at Kemble. Photograph L.R. Freeman, The Transport Treasury.

Below. 6822 MANTON GRANGE three minutes late at Kemble with the 5.28pm Cheltenham to Swindon semi-fast at 6.52pm. Leslie Freeman took the train after this, the infinitely preferable 7pm all stations Kemble-Swindon with four coaches behind pannier tank 4651, an engine which thoroughly belied the doubts of the Calne driver! Photograph L.R. Freeman, The Transport Treasury.

You'll Remember those Black and White Days...

Fourum
Watford Tunnel, South End, 14 April 1952

Black Five 44860 with an eight coach semi-fast (but note Class A headlamps) on the Up Fast Line just south of Watford Tunnel. The slow lines (to the right) are not visible from this spot. The loco is blowing off at the safety valves, so no doubt the regulator is shut for calling at Watford Junction. Photograph J.C. Flemons, The Transport Treasury.

Edge Hill's 46207 PRINCESS ARTHUR OF CONNAUGHT, immaculate in lined green livery, on an Up Liverpool-Euston express leaves the south end of Watford Tunnel – just seven coaches have emerged. Photograph J.C. Flemons, The Transport Treasury.

You'll Remember those Black and White Days...

Another Black Five, 45287, with Up Special W736 leaves the south end of Watford Tunnel. Note colour light signal for the Down Fast line at the tunnel mouth – almost certainly a distant signal. Photograph J.C. Flemons, The Transport Treasury.

Jubilee 45703 THUNDERER of 3B Bushbury heads the Up 'The Midlander' of eleven coaches. The Slow Lines to the right are now visible, showing well just how far apart the fast lines and slow line tunnels were. Note platelayer trolley and ballast bin and a lineside telephone. Photograph J.C. Flemons, The Transport Treasury.

You'll Remember those Black and White Days...

Yards Are Us!

Notes by Bryan Wilson
Photographs by George Heiron, courtesy Mrs
Shirley Heiron and The Transport Treasury

Above. The yards at Stoke Gifford, north of the city of Bristol; Up and Down yards were laid east of Filton Junction, on the north and south side respectively of the Badminton line. In the 1950s the Up 'Devonian' was the only Monday to Friday express for the Midland line to Birmingham that was routed via Filton Junction and Stoke Gifford. On Saturdays in high summer there were no less than twenty of them! And, it might be emphasised, the 'Devonian' only ran by this route in the Up direction. Trust George, therefore, to capture the train running through the middle of Stoke Gifford marshalling yards, behind Black 5 44856 of Derby and Jubilee 45573 NEWFOUNDLAND of Holbeck. On this nearest side there are two Down Goods adjacent to the Down Main, then ten sidings holding a variety of wagons. At a guess, those at the outward end of No.3 road are china clay empties for Cornwall, and many of the vans will be for Avonmouth. Note the loading gauge alongside No.10 road. This is where the Carriage & Wagon repairers might be performing and this gave them the means of checking dimensions of any adjusted loads or repaired wagons before releasing vehicles to traffic. Stoke Gifford dealt with services to and from London, Reading, Swindon, Oxford, Banbury and so on, as well as services from Washwood Heath and the Midland side after the demise of Westerleigh (Midland) sidings. Many through services also called here to attach and detach, particularly with traffic to and from Avonmouth.

Below right. A 'second chance' as George views the locomotives broadside on and, luckily for wagon enthusiasts, catches a GW 'Iron Mink' in the process. Built at the end of the Nineteenth Century it now serves as a SAND VAN 'for use at Stoke Gifford'. An 0-6-2T, 6670 of St Philips Marsh, lurks behind NEWFOUNDLAND.

You'll Remember those Black and White Days...

'The Devonian' on another day. This time the motive power is 44819 of Derby and local Jubilee 45660 ROOKE from Barrow Road shed. The Up side pannier tank pilot just gets in on the act.

Just to show the variety that Stoke Gifford once possessed. This time it's Britannia 70023 VENUS nicely turned out by Canton on an Up South Wales express. Eleven vehicles with effortless ease, including two nice GWR restaurant vehicles. The Up yard can be seen this time – an Up Goods Line and fourteen sidings. The Carriage & Wagon Dept. (and their loading gauge) occupy the two roads on the far side. Stoke Gifford church stands prominently behind the Up side wagons and Stoke Gifford West signal box can just be seen above the eighth coach. The yards closed on 4 October 1971 after which much of the site was covered by the new Bristol Parkway station with its car park and, more recently, the Royal Mail Depot which now has an uncertain future.

Now to central Bristol, to Pylle Hill at the west end of Temple Meads station – standing proud in the middle of the picture. To our left is Pylle Hill Goods Depot, a marshalling yard until West Depot came into use in 1915. Pylle Hill then dealt with full wagon loads of coal and goods plus livestock to and from the West of England. It also encompassed warehousing. In recent years, it had more to do with parcels traffic. Bath Road bridge is prominent and Bristol West signal box is the flat roofed building this side of it at the bottom of the stairway. Bath Road Diesel Depot is beyond the bridge with 'Loco Yard' box exactly opposite the Western diesel by the platform end. Through it all, a 'Hymek' Type 3 arrives with an Up train of mixed LM and WR stock.

You'll Remember those Black and White Days...

The heavenly and forgotten sight of the railway as prosperous and busy undertaking – this is 'East Depot' to the east of Temple Meads on the Bath line. It was a main yard for traffic to and from Reading, Salisbury, Weymouth, Chippenham, Westbury and so on, together with much local transfer traffic between Bristol yards and depots. It also made up loads of empties for Severn Tunnel Junction and Rogerstone in South Wales. We are looking towards Temple Meads; to our left is the Down Yard of seventeen roads and in the centre (from left to right) we have Down and Up Relief and Down and Up Main. Then comes Nos.1 and 2 Up Goods, followed by the eighteen road Up yard which had a 'hump' for gravitational shunting. The raised portion of line forming the 'hump' is bottom right, next to the tall ringed backing signal. A 350hp shunter stands alongside the fifteen lever Hump Cabin and another can just be seen in the 'spur' at the far end Down Yard by the elevated water tank. The coaches seen to the left in the distance are in Marsh Pond sidings by the Bristol avoiding line which goes off left beyond the loco exhaust in the distance ahead of us. And through it all comes one of St Philips Marsh's best, 6830 BUCKENHILL GRANGE with an up express.

You'll Remember those Black and White Days...

The wider view of 'East Depot' to the left, with a Down express passing through the middle of the yards and a pannier bringing a load of pipes on the Up Relief. A 94XX pannier sits in the middle of the Down Yard and the Up side 350hp shunter is still outside the cabin. The site ceased to function as a marshalling yard in August 1967 and has since become a home for Engineer's trains and defective wagons.

You'll Remember those Black and White Days...

Top left. We are now to the west, across the cold brown waters of the Bristol Channel. This is Wales, and the complex collection of lines and yards at Newport, South Wales. We are standing adjacent to the old Western Valleys line from Park Junction to Newport Dock Street at Maesglas Junction where that line crosses the South Wales main line. What a panorama! From left to right are Eastern Valley Sidings, New Sidings and Low Level Loop Sidings – thirty roads in all. The rear of West Mendalgief Signal Box can be seen on the high level former Newport (Alexandra Dock & Rly) line which crosses the main line on that large bridge, then progresses to the left along the embankment towards Mendalgief Sidings, Pill engine shed and the docks. The careful eye will notice one of the 9F 2-10-0s from the Ebbw Vale ore workings on the bridge proceeding to or from Ebbw Junction shed. Alexandra Dock Junction marshalling yard is to the left beyond the overbridge. A rare beast in the shape of Ebbw Junction's then sole 15XX, 1509, is stabled by the cabin in the 'V' between the Main lines and the Low Level Loop sidings. In the midst of all this glory, a Castle 4-6-0 passes Alexandra Dock Junction signal box and heads towards Cardiff with what looks like a service from Bristol.

Bottom left. While enjoying the view, a six car cross-country DMU passes on the Up Main with a Cardiff-Birmingham (Snow Hill) service, introduced in June 1957. A very clean 4913 BAGLAN HALL of Canton has arrived in the Up Loop with a Class 'H' train of 'best Welsh' steam coal. Ebbw Junction engine shed is just beyond the embankment to the right of the first overbridge.

Above. Lastly time moves on and 7014 CAERHAYS CASTLE is next on the Up Main with a Swansea-Bristol Temple Meads local. The variety of wagons on view in those sidings deserves a second look. The line from Park Junction to Ebbw Junction passes through the embankment by the bridge seen just to the right of the lighting pole.

You'll Remember those Black and White Days...

DieselDawn

network. It closed in April 1952 but continued in use as carriage sidings; a decision was made in 1955 to convert it to a diesel depot and work commenced in August 1955. This was a prelude to the introduction of Swindon-built, inter-city six car diesel multiple units on the Glasgow to Edinburgh via Falkirk diagrams. However, before these arrived a few Metro-Cammell sets were borrowed from the Eastern Region, for crew familiarisation and one is tempted to think that it is one of these that is being serviced in these views. Notice the Metro-Cammell 'Lot No.' plate, and date 1956, on the solebar. The lot number is 30190, and doubtless one of the more DMU-orientated readers can confirm that vehicles built to this Lot were, originally at least, allocated to the Eastern Region, and some of them were the sets loaned to the Scottish Region at this time. Answers to the Editor on a postcard please! Once open, the depot also had an allocation of diesel shunters, and the initial introduction of the Glasgow to Edinburgh diesel service started with a gradual replacement of steam, from 7 January 1957.

Leith Central was the first depot in the country to have the raised tracks and side pits, ideal for maintaining the first generation diesel multiple units. It

Lubricating at Leith – one of the most unusual and little-known Depots of the Diesel Era
Notes by Allan C Baker.

Three PR photographs, taken to further the sale of products by Tecalemit. This is still a well-known 'trade name' today for dispensing lubricants and other liquids. The pictures are taken inside Leith Central Diesel Depot, north-east of Edinburgh and, judging by the clean condition of the floor and pits, not long after it opened in

July 1956. This was an interesting Depot, unique in this country, as the building had formerly been a passenger station, Leith Central – the Leith Central branch of the North British had opened on 1 July 1903. The branch and its grandiose terminus never really delivered its promise and very soon fell victim to the ever-expanding local tram

Above. **A young fitter (it looks like a young Jim Gardener to me; Jim was an HQ technical guru, and an extremely good one, when I was in charge at Eastfield in the mid-1980s) uses the electric grease gun. The lubricant is fed in pipes to the radiator fan drive arrangements – that's the radiator to his right. Photograph courtesy The Transport Treasury.**

You'll Remember those Black and White Days...

prospered, and did not close until May 1972, when the remaining allocation was dispersed between Edinburgh Haymarket – which underwent some improvements to cater for an increased workload – Dundee and Glasgow Eastfield. This was all part of a quite major Regional scheme, to rationalise rolling stock maintenance. Leith Central had served the Region well; many a diesel set was, perforce, maintained in much, much inferior circumstances back in those early modernisation days of the 1950s, and indeed through to the 1960s.

Top. The complicated elephant trunk-like arrangement under the vehicle to drain the engine lubricating oil from the sump. Notice the belt drive to the radiator fan and generator; the circular 'pot' to the right is the vacuum exhauster lubricator – known to us as the 'vacuum pot'. Photograph courtesy The Transport Treasury.

Below. The sump of the AEC six cylinder horizontal engine is being refilled from a hand-operated barrel pump; observe the smart trolley complete with white walled tyres! Notice too, the legend 'Motive Power Dept Leith Central' painted on the trolley; the depot code was 64H by the way, a sub-shed of St Margarets and after closure of that shed, Haymarket. Photograph courtesy The Transport Treasury.

You'll Remember those Black and White Days...

Summer

Exeter Castle 5075 WELLINGTON leaves Brunel's Royal Albert Bridge and approaches Saltash station with an excursion to the Royal Duchy – Newquay as likely as not, around the summer of 1960. An improperly-dressed Fireman hands over the token as the train regains the double track. Over on the Devon side the embankment running below the woods carries the Southern main line. The bridge denotes the Ernesettle Establishment of the Royal Navy, in

Special...

which ammunition was stored both in surface buildings and in underground chambers. At one time it had standard gauge connections to the Southern line and its own internal narrow gauge, both serving a deep water jetty on the Tamar. It was said by locals, not without an element of perverse pride, to hold enough ammunition to blow up the whole of Plymouth...

Thanks to Ken Coventry and Eric Youldon.

You'll Remember those Black and White Days...

CONTINENTAL CORNER
Those Spanish Holidays
By Jack Hodgkinson

Nowadays a Spanish holiday for most Brits begins at Luton airport, or Gatwick, or whatever. My first excursion to Spain was on a more devious route – courtesy of H M. Aircraft-Carrier 'Implacable' into Gibraltar, a change into 'civvies' in the snooker-room of the military barracks, then a bus ride to the frontier of La Linea. My second visit was more refined, by Royal Mail Line steamer 'Alcantara' out of Southampton bent on a Mediterranean cruise. My pal and I paid £10 each for the privilege of a one-way fare to the first port of call – La Coruna – then we went coast to coast via Madrid on the R.E.N.F.E. network.

Thereafter it was the tedious business of the boat train from London Victoria, the ferry to France via Dover or Folkestone (fingers crossed that it wasn't a French vessel) the boat train to Paris Nord, a Metro ride across the capital, and the overnight sleeper from Gare d'Austerlitz to Irun or Port-Bou. Port-Bou was the favourite (when with my family) as the gateway to the Costa Brava, Barcelona or points further south. On solo trips, Irun was the starting point for the Basque country and the remaining steam spots on the more northerly plains.

There were two major differences between our own shores and the Iberian Peninsula. Firstly, the broad gauge of 5ft 6ins immediately made itself felt, in the close-up dimensions of the larger locomotive types. Second was the archaic timetable which, year after year, enabled you to get to some desired location but often didn't allow you to get back on the same day. One obvious blessing was the weather – sunshine wasn't guaranteed but was present more often than not – which elevated the success rate on your exposures.

Unlike visits to British steam depots where you could get round with the 'nod' from a friendly foreman, I always approached their Spanish counterparts with authority from Madrid H.Q.* I have been 'jumped on' both front and rear by armed police but frowns turned to smiles on production of the little 'yellow card' declaring permission to visit and obtain photographs. It was often the signal to be offered a cigarette, or a swig from a leathern wine flask!

Steam power lingered on in Spain well after its demise here in 1968, helping to soften the blow. The extra incentive to make Spain a holiday destination, where it could be sampled without too much effort, was obvious. Fortunately the Spanish have made great efforts on the preservation scene, by museum exhibitions, heritage rail sites, plinthed locos, and some working steam for chartered runs. If you didn't see Spanish steam in its heyday, you can still get quite a good run for your money.

*I did try it on ONCE. I asked for the 'JEFE' (Chief) at Tarragona, and was ushered into a smoke-filled sanctum. The sun blinds were drawn, the atmosphere smoke-laden from about six men seated – all smoking cigars. It must have been the morning conference. In my halting Spanish I explained who I was, and what I wanted. The Chief listened attentively then pronounced me free to wander the depot – BUT – I must leave my camera with him. He was just afraid that pictures might get published without Madrid's authority!

Above. SNCF American 141R 2-8-2 No.836 on arrival at Port Bou, 10 May 1966. The 5ft 6in gauge rails are to the right. Inside the cathedral-like station it used to be a real hub-bub when 'the overnights' arrived, disgorging their swarms of returning Nationals and eager holidaymakers. There were French and Spanish customs officials delving into luggage, dual passport checks and, during occasional epidemic scares, vaccination certificates were demanded. Unlucky travellers without such a document were herded together and marched to a 'medico' for a jab – like it or not. Today's scene is so different. Documentation is no longer required and with the place more or less deserted you can hear a pin drop. Photograph Jack Hodgkinson.

A brace of 141s under repair at Campo Sepulcro workshops, Zaragoza, 21 March 1969. Photograph Jack Hodgkinson.

The business side of things on 241-2102 at Miranda de Ebro, 16 December 1969. They were very unfairly nick-named 'bath tubs' by British fans. Photograph Jack Hodgkinson.

You'll Remember those Black and White Days...

240-2584 climbs out of Castejon de Ebro, bound for Pamplona, 27 April 1968. Photograph Jack Hodgkinson.

241-4067 waits for the off at Miranda de Ebro, 26 April 1968 after taking over a Bilbao-Logrono train. it had been built by Babcock & Wilcox in 1946. Photograph Jack Hodgkinson.

Esta autorización es personal e intransferible.
El titular está obligado a justificar su personalidad con el Documento Nacional de Identidad, Carnet ferroviario o Pasaporte.
Deberá someterse a las indicaciones que le haga el personal de la Red Nacional, con el fín de no perturbar el buen servicio de la misma.
RENFE no responde de ninguna clase de perjuicios que puedan ocasionarse al titular, que firma a continuación.

Jack Hodgkinson

(Firma del interesado)

CONCESIONES	DEPENDENCIAS O INSTALACIONES
Visita y obtención de fotografías.	Depósitos, Reservas y estaciones de ALSASUA, MIRANDA, CASTEJÓN, PANCORBO y SAN FELICES

Cars by Southern to the West
By Eric Youldon

On 8 September 1962 34109 SIR TRAFFORD LEIGH-MALLORY has the 8.03am Car Carrier descending Exeter bank. Photograph A.E. West.

It all started in 1958. That summer the Southern Region advertised a car carrying service of sorts from Nine Elms to Exeter or Barnstaple, on all days except Sundays. Motorists were invited to drive to Nine Elms Depot between 8.0am and 5.0pm for their cars to be placed in covered vans and conveyed by overnight freight train to Exeter Central Station Yard or Barnstaple Junction Station Yard. Drivers were reminded that a frequent service of electric trains ran between Vauxhall and Waterloo (in case they didn't know!) from where they could journey on any one of a selection of scheduled services to Exeter (seven trains) or Barnstaple (five trains). Extra trains were available on Saturdays and similar arrangements applied in the up direction. Car drivers were instructed to hand over their ignition keys to the railway representative when parting from their cars at Nine Elms, Exeter or Barnstaple.

A typical charge, second class, was £8-5-0 return to Exeter with £2-6-0 for each additional passenger plus £1-3-0 per child. The same

operation was repeated the following year but from summer 1960 the more familiar Surbiton to Okehampton Car Carrier was inaugurated. This

was a dedicated service consisting of coaches and vans for the motorist, his family and his car. Passengers and cars were loaded in

Light Pacific 34089 602 SQUADRON passing Exmouth Junction shed (the coaling plant is on the right) with the up Car Carrier in 1962. Photograph George Powell, Great Eastern Railway Society Collection.

You'll Remember those Black and White Days...

DAY CAR/CARRIER SERVICE
SURBITON—OKEHAMPTON : SATURDAYS

	SATURDAYS 30th May, 6th June, 13th June and 12th September	SATURDAYS 20th June to 5th September, inclusive
Surbiton ..dep	8 03 am	8 03 am
Okehampton arr	12 28 pm	12 26 pm
Okehampton dep	3 08 pm	3 55 pm
Surbiton ..arr	7 15 pm	8 11 pm

Fares *

	Single	Return
Driver and Car	£10 10 0	£17 0 0
Additional Passengers	2 6 6	4 13 0
Children age 3 and under 14	1 3 3	2 6 6

★ A Peak Surcharge is made on outward journeys from 25th July to 29th August inclusive - Driver and Car £1 10 0 single £3 0 0 return.

WATERLOO—EXETER (CENTRAL) : SUNDAYS

SUNDAYS: 31st May to 6th September, inclusive
Waterloo .. dep   9 00 am
Exeter Central arr   12 50 pm

SUNDAYS: 31st May to 13th September, inclusive
Exeter Central dep   4 12 pm
Waterloo .. arr   7 49 pm

Fares

	Single	Return
Driver and Car	£9 10 0	£15 0 0
Additional Passengers	2 3 0	4 6 0
Children age 3 and under 14	1 1 6	2 3 0

For reservations and further information apply to the Line Manager, South Western Division, 19 Worple Road, Wimbledon, S.W.19.

ISLE OF WIGHT CAR FERRIES

If you are thinking of going to the Isle of Wight with your car, we provide regular Car Ferry services between Portsmouth and Fishbourne, also between Lymington and Yarmouth.

For details ask at Enquiry Offices for the "Isle of Wight Car Ferry Folder" or write to the Central Reservation Office, Isle of Wight Car Ferry Services, 102, Broad Street, Portsmouth, Hampshire; telephone Portsmouth 22571.

The only time that the Car Carrier appeared in the public timetable was in this summer issue for 1964. Note the Sunday service from Waterloo to Exeter Central by ordinary train.

You'll Remember those Black and White Days...

the down side yard at Surbiton on separate tracks with the vans shunted on to the front of the coaches. On arrival at Okehampton cars and passengers were offloaded in the military sidings a short distance beyond the station. The second class fare for driver and vehicle was £12 (later increased to £15 and finally by 1964 to £17) plus a supplement for each additional passenger. First class fares were also available.

Initially a formation comprising a three coach set and seven GUVs (general utility vans) was assigned to the train but starting in the summer of 1961 demand warranted an additional van and a restaurant car replaced one of the carriages, giving an eleven vehicle train with room for 24 cars. Roof boards were displayed throughout the train proclaiming 'Surbiton-Okehampton Car Carrier Train', and it ran on all Saturdays in the 1960 Summer timetable.

The Car Carrier was a success so the Southern, in a fit of exuberance and doubtless keen to make greater use of its new train set, extended the operation in the summer of 1961

to include Fridays and Sundays. Enthusiasm cooled a little after this so that the summers of 1962 and 1963 saw the Carrier running on Fridays and Saturdays only and by 1964, the final year, it was back to being a Saturdays only service. However, in that last year some compensation was afforded by attaching vans, with cars loaded at Waterloo, to the front of the 9.0am ordinary train to Exeter Central where the cars were taken off. A similar working to Waterloo, using the same vans and coaches, departed from Exeter Central at 4.12pm.

In practice the Friday and Sunday Surbitons were a disappointment; when they ran they were poorly patronised and frequently cancelled. *The Railway Observer* reported that the up train on Friday 28 July 1961 ran empty direct to Clapham Junction where the stock was based. On at least one Sunday in 1961 when demand was low two vans, for just four cars, were attached to an ordinary service and presumably detached at Okehampton. The Saturday trains fared much better and some years were extended to

include certain Saturdays preceding or following the period of the summer timetable.

Typical Saturday schedules for the Car Carrier showed a departure from Surbiton at 8.3am with an engine charge on the down through road at Exeter Central from 11.30 to 11.39am giving an arrival at Okehampton at 12.26pm. Return was at 3.55pm from Okehampton and, with an engine change on the up through road at Exeter Central from 4.34 to 4.39pm, finished the day at Surbiton at 8.11pm. A stop was made at Salisbury both ways for the locomotive to take water.

On arriving at Okehampton the Carrier proceeded through the station and halted clear of the trailing crossover whereupon the Pacific was detached. The station shunter, typically an 'N' 2-6-0, then coupled to the rear and drew the train forward over the crossover into the up platform from where a further reversal saw the train propelled alongside the long military platform for cars to emerge via the end loading dock. The three coaches were pulled off and shunted into the short platform for passengers to alight. For

the return service the Pacific, after turning and servicing at the shed, shunted the coaches with returning passengers on the loaded vans and set off up the line.

Motive Power from Surbiton was usually a Nine Elms Merchant Navy as far as Exeter Central which returned on the 2.30pm to Waterloo. Continuation westwards was, with rare exceptions, behind an Exmouth Junction light Pacific. For the up working from Exeter to Surbiton haulage was typically a Nine Elms Merchant Navy again although the final year frequently produced a small Pacific, the engine having previously come down earlier on the 9.0am from Waterloo to East Devon as far as Sidmouth Junction. An interesting variation occurred on 13 June 1964 when BR Standard Fives were to the fore; 73115 of Nine Elms arrived at Exeter Central with the down train and gave way to Exmouth Junction's 73030.

The last day the Surbiton ran was Saturday 12 September 1964 when West Country Pacific No.34046 BRAUNTON worked down to Exeter. So ended a commendable example of Southern enterprise that saw staff handing publicity leaflets to motorists in traffic jams around Exeter. Henceforth the Western Region, now in command throughout the West, decreed that such traffic would in future be confined to their traditional territory.

Grateful thanks to Alistair Jeffrey for help with train times, and to Arthur Westlake for Okehampton details.

Left. Light Pacific 34056 CROYDON with the 8.03am down train, on Fatherford viaduct near Okehampton, Saturday 30 July 1960. Photograph S.C. Nash.

Below. Last season of the Car Carrier, a Saturday in August 1964. Cars wait to load on to the up working at Okehampton, leaving for Surbiton at 3.55pm. In the background are the passenger coaches waiting to be shunted on to the train. Photograph J. Holland.

You'll Remember those Black and White Days...

FOURUM Wood Green, 27 March 1954

Notes by Peter Coster ('I particularly like the WD shot. You can almost hear the old thing clanking along. It looks as though the driver is letting the boy have a turn at driving')

Copley Hill A1 60120 KITTIWAKE passes beneath the New Line Flyover with the 13.18 West Riding express. Tunnel box was behind the camera, Tunnel sidings were on both sides of the four running lines, and the independent Down Goods ran west of the flyover approach, locally known as the Khyber Pass. To the right were the old brickfields, where the bricks for the tunnel were made. March 27th 1954 was a fairly average Saturday, a 'V2 day' when several Green Arrows replaced the usual Pacifics on several duties. Photograph R. Wilson, The Transport Treasury.

Nearer the station, A3 No.60039 SANDWICH is on the 15.10 to Newcastle, returning to her home shed at Grantham. This was normally a top link A1 duty. The foreground track is the down slow, and one can see the double crossovers whereby Wood Green No.3 could reroute a Down Slow No.1 train to Enfield, and a Down Slow No.2 train to the main line. The bright white post in front of the A3, unlike the others carrying signal wires, marks a section of track proposed for renewal. Photograph R. Wilson, The Transport Treasury.

The J6 0-6-0s had a soft exhaust which belied their good turn of speed, and were often used north of Peterborough on passenger turns. For a few magic weeks, New England had to turn to their J6s in place of WDs for some reason, and one could see them with surprisingly long trains of coal empties pounding north. But, oh that Spartan cab! Without doubt, 64266, at Hornsey for many years, has spent the day at New Southgate as pilot, and is making her way back to shed. As it is a Saturday, there is no traffic or empty coal wagons from the gas works. Photograph R. Wilson, The Transport Treasury.

A class H unbraked goods creeps out of Wood Green tunnel on the Up Slow, behind WD 90428. It is a superb shot of one of New England's long-term WD fleet, emerging into the sunshine. For that reason I am suspicious of the date since the other three shots suggest a typical neutral March day. But how we groaned as yet *another* WD plodded southwards, the motion usually clanking and the snifting valve chinking. No state of neglect seemed too appalling, they just carried on. The WD brakes were not good, and most drivers seemed wary of letting the speed rise too much lest they get pushed past where they needed to stop. Photograph R. Wilson, The Transport Treasury.

You'll Remember those Black and White Days...

Scenic Southall

On 26 April 1952 7014 CAERHAYS CASTLE, a Newton Abbot engine, approaches the famous footbridge at Southall (it led to the engine shed over on the right). It is on the Down Main with the 1.15pm Paddington-Weston-Super-Mare. Photograph J.C. Flemons, The Transport Treasury.

You'll Remember those Black and White Days...

The rest of these studies at sunny Southall, famous for its beaches and palm trees, were taken a week or so earlier than the one opposite, on 12 April 1952, from the well-known footbridge or close to it, and are presented in time order. First up is 7919 RUNTER HALL piloting another Hall on the 10.45am Paddington-Cheltenham approaching Southall station. The time is 11am and the photographer is standing on the Up Main platform. Note the sheer quantity of point rodding between Up and Down Main Lines, as well as GWR ATC ramp on Up Main Line. Evidence of 'spotters' on that footbridge... Photograph J.C. Flemons, The Transport Treasury.

Five minutes on it's 11.35am with a Castle on the Up Main Line with the 4.55am Fishguard-Paddington Boat Train, approaching Southall station with eleven coaches. This view is from the road bridge – Southall Gas Works is to the right with the Down Goods Yard behind the train. Photograph J.C. Flemons, The Transport Treasury.

You'll Remember those Black and White Days...

Another two minutes on 12 April 1952 and a 2-6-2T, 6127, rattles by at 11.37am with 10.30am Reading-Paddington seven coach local. View again is from the road bridge. Note pointwork and ground signals in foreground. The building to the left is the Staff Hostel. Photograph J.C. Flemons, The Transport Treasury.

High noon on 12 April and 6125 of Southall shed heads the 11.30am Slough-Paddington five coach local – we are almost certainly witnessing a crew change. Two blokes walk down the ramp (this was the walking route across to the shed via a timber crossing). On the Up Relief 2-8-0 3851 (no smokebox number plate) stands on the Down Relief waiting to cross to the shed. To the right is the Bay Platform with an 0-6-0PT just visible – probably shunting parcel vans. 'Southall Castle' (actually a water tower!) is just visible in the murk with gasometer beyond. Photograph J.C. Flemons, The Transport Treasury.

At 12.40pm we get 6169 (in plain black livery) on a five coach local, the 12.07pm ex-Paddington running late, on the Down Relief line. Goods shed and yard to the rear. Photograph J.C. Flemons, The Transport Treasury.

Finally, a mere nine minutes on at 12.49pm, Bath Road's lined black 6977 GRUNDISBURGH HALL comes by on the Down Relief line with a milk train. Southall truly was scenic! Photograph J.C. Flemons, The Transport Treasury.

You'll Remember those Black and White Days...

FOURUM Canute Road Crossing

Entry to, or exit from, the Old or Eastern Docks at Southampton involved crossing the sometimes busy Canute Road. There were no traffic lights provided to halt the road traffic, merely a warning sign TRAINS CROSS HERE as may be seen in the picture of the BR Class 4 2-6-0 76016 making its way across. All these photographs were taken by H.C. Casserley in May 1957 and at that time the twelve wheel Pullman car MYRTLE was an unclassed car with a buffet and

carried the roofboards WATERLOO SOUTHAMPTON DOCKS which suggests it was part of a Channel Islands set rather than an Ocean Liner train. The M7 0-4-4T 30356 is probably working empty stock. In the picture of 34044 WOOLACOMBE the flagman in his regulation waistcoat is prominent with his flag.
Notes by D.W. Winkworth.

LONDON TERMINI UNDER ATTACK

Southwark Road bridge outside Blackfriars station in June 1941. The miracle of these dark times was the speed and purpose of the way things were made to function afterwards. Observe how one girder has been left in place, despite being buckled and battered, while temporary supports have been laid in on the other side.

Holborn Viaduct in April 1941. The station had been badly affected by incendiaries late the previous year and presumably this is the result of a subsequent attack, a bomb having reduced this building to shell. Those drunken walls will have to be demolished before the lines can open again.

You'll Remember those Black and White Days...

WAR REPORT ... WAR REPORT ... WA

These two sorry scenes are at Charing Cross in 1940. We do not have the exact date though it is fairly safe to assume that this is 'the morning after' or even the 'afternoon after' a daylight raid on central London which took place on the morning of 8 October 1940. The main casualty was the EMU in Platform 5 and the W.H. Smith bookstall opposite the bomb which tore apart that carriage. The wonder is that the stall survives at all – there are papers and magazines still littering the counter but these have probably been gathered up and plonked there as the clear-up got underway. The station is clearly not yet open to passengers – but will be soon.

You'll Remember those Black and White Days...

Mr. Dixon's Polloc and Govan Railway Some Ancient History

Robert M. Grogans

It is impossible, of course, to illustrate the ancient Pollac & Govan, so we must rely on fragments, the 'air' of the line as it were, such as are available in much later modern day scenes. As here – this is West Street Junction, on the goods line from Larkfield Junction to Shields Junction, which connected the Rutherglen and Paisley routes, on a busy summer Saturday morning, 29 June 1957. The view is from the bridge carrying the Cathcart Circle and Barrhead lines, with BR Class 5 4-6-0 No.73010 on the 9.25am Heads of Ayr-Edinburgh Princes Street. Caley 'Jumbo' 0-6-0 No.57278 is in the mineral depot loop with a freight. On the left Black Five No.44886 with a Clyde Coast relief from Lanarkshire coalfield stations takes water and changes crew. To the right the sidings lie on the course of the Polloc & Govan Railway. Photograph W.A.C. Smith.

Britain's railway system owed much to the old wagonways or tramways. These early 'railroads' primarily linked the coal mines of eighteenth century and early nineteenth century Britain to the nearest river, canal or coastal outlet for transportation to the markets. Although they were far less numerous than their English counterparts, the Scottish wagonways were built for similar purposes. Most were short to medium in length, but elaborate schemes were proposed from time to time that were never constructed.

One of these, in the early 1800s, was a proposal to link Berwick-upon-Tweed with Glasgow and connect the Tweed salmon and Northumbrian fisheries with the rapidly growing industrial conurbation in Glasgow and greater Clydeside. It had also been intended to pass through the Borders agricultural, woollen and textile areas to tap into these local markets. Another project was planned to link Glasgow with Greenock on the Clyde estuary. However, the arrival of steam

locomotive traction on the Stockton and Darlington Railway by 1825 soon changed the thinking behind such projects.

In Glasgow wagonways linked several coal mines with their main outlet, the River Clyde. During the 1770s, and certainly by 1780, two

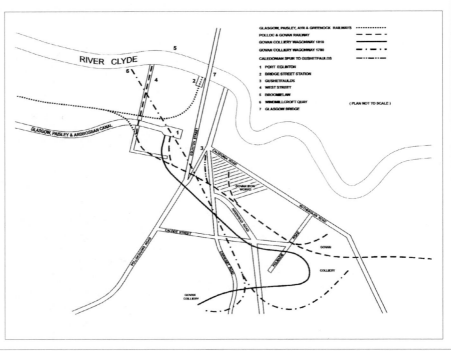

wagonways were of particular importance. One linked coal mines on the north bank of the river in Knightswood with Yoker, on the riverside opposite the burgh of Renfrew on the south bank. The other, believed to have been constructed between 1775 and 1778, linked Govan Colliery in modern-day Govanhill with the Clyde at Windmillcroft, opposite the city's Broomielaw quay. Quays on the south bank were often described by nineteenth century writers as part of the Broomielaw quay despite its location on the north bank of the river.

One nineteenth century plan shows the line of the wagonway in 1780 as exiting from the Govan Colliery pits, cutting over what is modern-day Cathcart Road, then running parallel with that thoroughfare before cutting back over it and progressing in a diagonal north-westerly direction over Eglinton Street and West Street, before it terminated at the Govan Coal Company's quay at Windmillcroft.

The importance of both wagonways were that they were financed by merchants Colin Dunlop and Alexander Houston and their successors, who owned the coal companies that mined in each location. By the late eighteenth century both the Houston and Dunlop trading interests had

suffered from business collapse and by the early nineteenth century the Knightswood Coal Company had fallen under the majority control of a John Dixon and his sons. By then they were the major partners and they also managed and later owned a very successful glassworks in the town of Dumbarton, further west on the north bank of the river.

By 1790 the Govan Coal Company had come under the managing control of Dixon's nephew William Dixon, who in 1806 assumed ownership as one of a seven-strong business partnership. By 1813 William Dixon was the sole owner of the Govan Coal Company as well as other coal mines and an iron works in Calder near Coatbridge in the Monklands of Lanarkshire. During his early years as manager of the Govan coal works he was instrumental in improving the colliery wagonway links with the Clyde. One contemporary historian has described the regular flow of wooden-built wagons trundling down to the riverside, tended by workmen and hauled by horses when necessary.

The Dixons had came north from Tyneside around 1770 and were well-versed in the techniques of coal extraction and transportation. The commercial opportunities afforded by the demise of the Houston and Dunlop families, crippled as they were by the disruption to the West

Indian mercantile and slave trades caused by war and rebellion, allowed the Dixons to gradually succeed to ownership. Predominantly it was glass manufacture on the part of John Dixon and his sons, and coal mining and iron production in the case of his nephew, William Dixon. Their respective paths to industrial and commercial success then deviated, and while the successors of old John Dixon eventually saw their fortunes crumble due to an acrimonious family squabble by the late 1830s, those of William Dixon and his sons went from strength to strength.

In 1811 a canal was opened that was originally intended to link the south side of Glasgow with the town and port of Ardrossan on the North Ayrshire coast of the Firth of Clyde. Seen partly as a way of circumventing the River Clyde and the charges levied by the river's Glasgow-based trustees, the canal was never constructed beyond the Renfrewshire town of Johnstone. It was in effect a man-made and land-locked waterway. The development of the embryonic railways would make it virtually obsolete within two decades of its opening.

William Dixon, in 1808, prior to the canal's opening, had pushed forward plans to construct a new wagonway from the colliery to the canal's Glasgow terminus at Port Eglinton. The Govan Coal Company

The Polloc & Govan Railway was transformed out of all recognition – here it is in the late summer of 1963, from Polmadie Road bridge – the mighty shed is on the left. Jubilee 45613 KENYA heads the 9.10am local from Carlisle to Glasgow Central on 13 September 1963. Photograph W.A.C. Smith.

You'll Remember those Black and White Days...

Section from a typical nineteenth century 'overview' – Glasgow around 1864. At the bottom centre of the illustration is West Street with the tracks of the Polloc & Govan Railway still in place at that time. To the bottom right Bridge Street station is clearly illustrated. Courtesy The Illustrated London News Picture Library.

You'll Remember those Black and White Days...

In March 1961 46107 ARGYLL & SUTHERLAND HIGHLANDER makes heavy weather of an admittedly lengthy train of mineral empties past Dalmarnock, Rutherglen. Rutherglen was the terminus of the Polloc & Govan Railway but eventually became a through stopping point after the Clydesdale Junction Railway was built by William Dixon Jnr, thus extending the old Polloc & Govan Railway. Photograph W.A.C. Smith.

had planned a coal quay at Port Eglinton and had also purchased land upon which to construct the wagonway and to complete the link with the colliery. Much of the wagonway route ran close to the older line to Windmillcroft. But in order to connect with Port Eglinton the wagonway had to cross Pollokshaws Road, a thoroughfare which linked areas south of the river with the city itself, and close to prestige property developments.

Before Dixon could complete the link over the road, David Laurie, a Glasgow property developer, took legal action. He had persuaded the Sheriff's office in Glasgow to serve an interdict preventing Dixon from building his wagonway across Pollokshaws Road. He was alarmed that its construction threatened his property interests south of the River Clyde. These were targeted to appeal to the growing middle class population seeking suitable accommodation south of the river. Laurie feared that the land and the properties already constructed would be devalued and his financial investments greatly harmed.

What he had not reckoned on was a determined William Dixon, by then the main driving force behind the success of the Govan Coal Company and the sprawling Govan Colliery in an area which was then known as Little Govan. He was no slouch when it came to protecting his substantial and continually growing coal markets. Transport to and from these was essential and the newly constructed canal was expected to prove a boon in cutting costs for the supply of many of the company's customers – as indeed it was, for several years after it had opened.

To overcome Laurie's opposition, Dixon and his lawyers presented a case that persuaded the Sheriff to lift the interdict, on a Saturday just prior to the closure of the Sheriff's office for business until the following Monday. Objective achieved, Dixon, who had squads of workmen and materials at the ready, immediately set about the completion of the wagonway across Pollokshaws Road. His men worked non-stop throughout the weekend and completed the task. By the time

Laurie had discovered what had happened, and the Sheriff's offices had reopened for business on the Monday he was far too late to change matters.

The rest was history, to use an old cliché. Dixon and Laurie argued their spat out in the courts after that, but Dixon prevailed. While his wagonway greatly aided the growth and profitability of the coal company in the years that followed, Laurie suffered badly. His dream of a middle class garden suburb stretching over much of what was then Glasgow's south side was soundly shattered. So too was much of the value of the land and the property in the area owned or leased by him. When middle class housing development took off in a big way south of the River Clyde, it did so during the 1860s and 1870s on the lands of the newly formed burghs of Crosshill and Govanhill, the majority of which, ironically, was owned and feued out by Dixon's grandson, William Smith Dixon.

William Dixon died in October 1822. He left to his two surviving sons, John and William, the then largest coal mining and iron working business empire in Scotland. William Dixon Jnr. bought out his brother's share of that inheritance several years later. In time he built upon his father's foundations and gradually increased the property and financial holdings of William Dixon and Company. One of his key strategies during the period between 1825 and 1850 was to encourage and invest in the growing influence of railway construction, initially on Clydeside. His early interests were solely for the purpose of creating what would nowadays be termed mineral railways.

He was involved in a number of schemes, particularly in and around the Lanarkshire coalfield. The Ballochney Railway, the Wishaw and Coltness Railway, and more importantly the Monkland and Kirkintilloch Railway, were all subject to his support. The latter was seen by Dixon and others as a tool to upset the monopoly enjoyed by the Monkland Canal Company in the transportation of coal and iron to the Glasgow markets. The Monkland and Kirkintilloch provided a valuable link from the Monkland coalfield to the Forth and Clyde Canal basin at Kirkintilloch, thus undercutting the Monkland Canal's dominance.

Within the city of Glasgow William Dixon Jnr. was also active in railway promotion. The plan to link the Broomielaw harbour on the city's north bank of the River Clyde with the Forth and Clyde and Monkland canals at the Port Dundas basin on the northern outskirts of the city

met with his enthusiastic support. Promoted in 1829, when £200,000 of capital for the project had been raised, Dixon was elected on to a steering committee which had to 'sell' the project to a number of wary and hostile parties. In the event the planned railway failed to materialise, primarily due to the proposal that the major segment of the route should be tunnelled under the Blythswood lands which lay between the two stretches of water.

This was populated by the wealthy and powerful middle class strata of Glasgow society and fears that their smart and palatial city homes would collapse and disappear into the cavernous tunnel beneath fuelled their opposition to the project.

Dixon was also an avid supporter of the first truly designated mineral and passenger steam traction railway in Scotland, the Garnkirk and Glasgow Railway, which proved to be the catalyst for railway development in and around the city. He is also most likely to have been a supporter for the 1834 plan for a double track tramway along Broomielaw Quay from Jamaica Street on the eastern edge to slightly beyond Warroch Street on the western edge. Slightly west of centre of the proposed tramway a weighing machine for wagons was to be located, nestled amid a network of junctions and crossovers. The intended use of steam traction was evident by the location of ashpits at regular intervals as noted on the plans. Like the tunnel railway project the Broomielaw tramway was never constructed.

Dixon's enthusiasm for railways can be assessed by the various shares he held with the Monkland and Kirkintilloch, the Wishaw and Coltness, and the Garnkirk and Glasgow railway companies. He also gave practical and financial support for the Edinburgh and Glasgow

Nothing could be further, even from the far-sighted Dixon's dreams – 46229 DUCHESS OF HAMILTON at Rutherglen with the up Royal Scot on the old Polloc & Govan route, 24 September 1960. Photograph W.A.C. Smith.

Railway, and when the Caledonian Railway Company was formed Dixon was on the provisional committee and held twenty shares, having subscribed £1,000 toward its formation.

Over the ensuing years he built up a significant shareholding in several railway ventures. When his son, William Smith Dixon died in 1880, his will showed a number of railway shareholdings that he had inherited from his father. These included shares in the Glasgow, Bothwell & Coatbridge Railway Company, the Caledonian Railway Company, the Greenock Railway Company, the Girvan & Portpatrick Junction Railway Company and even abroad with the Mexican Railway Company. Proof indeed that William Dixon Jnr. clearly participated during the various bouts of railway mania.

But among all of his railway ventures his *piece de resistance* was arguably the development of his own Polloc and Govan and later Clydesdale Junction railways. Dixon foresaw a great advantage through the use of steam locomotion in linking his colliery at Little Govan and other collieries in Rutherglen and parts of Lanarkshire. That included Calder, where he continued to operate the successful Calder Iron Works. The first phase of that plan was to promote the Polloc and

Govan Railway, which was virtually an upgrading of the Port Eglinton wagonway and extend the route of it down to the River Clyde where it terminated at a coal quay at the foot of West Street in the district of modern-day Tradeston.

William Dixon, Jnr. had to fight considerable opposition from interests on Glasgow City Council opposed to his plans. That opposition may have fuelled his move to seek election to the city council for the Gorbals ward, which he had achieved by 1833. It took several more years to develop the Polloc and Govan and it was on 22 August 1840 that the railway was finally opened.

The Polloc and Govan Railway Act was passed on May 1830, and in easing its passage through parliament, Dixon rented office space in the House of Commons at Westminster for himself and his legal representatives so that they could be on hand to smooth out and overcome any objections or obstacles that invariably arose. During the ensuing ten years that it took to open, the original plan to construct the line from Govan Colliery down to the River Clyde at West Street, Tradeston, and a branch to the Port Eglinton basin of the Glasgow, Paisley and Ardrossan Canal was supplemented with an

extension to Rutherglen which was authorised in 1831. By 1837 an extension of time had been granted for the construction of the line. The opening was achieved close to the expiry of the Act's extension, and the branch to Port Eglinton was opened slightly later.

The newspaper, the *Glasgow Courier,* described the opening day of the Polloc and Govan Railway in August 1840 by noting that it had been opened, *...from Rutherglen to the Broomielaw Harbour, on Saturday the 22d inst., with a train of carriages containing the son of the spirited proprietor, Wm. Dixon, Esq. of Govanhill, and friends, the engineer and contractors upon the line, and also of trains of coal wagons. Considerable exertions were required to complete this line within the time limited by the Act - 2,100 lineal yards of this railway having been laid down within four days. On this line is to be seen every species of railroad engineering, - tunnelling, right-angled and skew bridges, of stone, brick, iron, and wood, all of which do credit to the engineer, Mr. Andrew Thomson, Buchanan Street, Glasgow. The whole opening went off with great eclat under the direction of Mr. Allan, manager of Govan Colliery. The colliery band, who had volunteered their services, contributed very much to enliven the proceedings of the day. The* *contemplated extension of this line of railway, with a terminus at the Broomielaw Harbour, to the Monkland, Wishaw, Coltness and Hamilton coal and ironstone fields, will render it one of the most available means of opening up the richest district in Scotland.*

A few weeks prior to the opening of the Polloc and Govan William Dixon Jnr. was one of the 160 gentlemen guests who sat down to a celebratory dinner in the fashionable Tontine Hotel, Glasgow on Monday July 13, 1840 to mark the opening of the Glasgow and Paisley Railway. Dixon's presence at that dinner further indicated his enthusiasm for railways, and a flurry of Acts of Parliament before and after the opening of the Polloc and Govan saw his eager support for rail links that benefited his production and trading interests.

After the Polloc and Govan had been opened it was quickly connected in the ensuing years with the Glasgow, Paisley, Kilmarnock and Ayr (Joint) Railway, and the Glasgow, Paisley and Greenock Railway. The latter in particular was subject to Dixon's constant vocal and financial support and virtually became his crusade to offset what he saw as the punitive harbourage charges levied by the Clyde River Trustees, an affront to his political belief in the right of free trade.

As early as 1839 he had plans drawn up to link the Polloc and Govan with the Edinburgh and Glasgow and the Garnkirk and Glasgow Railways. These two connections were proposed by means of a spur from the Polloc and

Govan near Polmadie and then on through Rutherglen to cross the River Clyde north of Shawfield Toll, through the Dalmarnock and Bridgeton districts before linking with the two railways north of the river.

Dixon vigorously promoted for an Act of Parliament to construct the Clydesdale Junction Railway and the Act was successfully passed in 1845. The Act allowed for a railway to be constructed from the Polloc and Govan Railway's eastern terminus at Horsecroft in Rutherglen to Hamilton, with a branch from Park Farm in Cambuslang to connect with the Wishaw and Coltness Railway, near Motherwell. The Act also included an allowance for branches in Tradeston from the Polloc and Govan to make the links with the Glasgow, Paisley, Kilmarnock and Ayr (Joint) and the Glasgow, Paisley and Greenock railways. Dixon eventually had sidings and coal terminals built at both Paisley and Greenock once he had connected the Polloc and Govan to these lines.

Both the Polloc and Govan and Clydesdale Junction Railways required painstaking and legally laborious but undoubtedly financially lucrative work on the part of Dixon's solicitors, with regard to the purchase and lease of hundreds of plots of land through which these railways traversed. But his status as one of Scotland's leading iron and coal producers had made him a very rich man, so finance was not problem as he drove ahead with his ambitious railway plans.

That wealth allowed him to draw heavily on loans from the Scottish banks and he was in effect the sole owner and shareholder of the Polloc and Govan and also by far the largest shareholder in the Clydesdale Junction Railway which finally linked his Lanarkshire coal and iron interests. Eventually the newly-founded Caledonian Railway Company bought up a number of smaller concerns. In 1846 the Polloc & Govan was acquired by the Caledonian, who had also acquired Dixon's Clydesdale Junction line. He also sold land at Gushetfaulds where the Caledonian was to build its then main Glasgow terminus, South Side Station.

Dixon made a considerable profit in his dealings with the Caledonian which became, arguably, Scotland's leading railway company in later years. Not only did he profit through the sales of his railway holdings, he also gained as a shareholder when the Caledonian was able to expand steadily and increase profitability thanks to acquisitions from individuals such as himself.

In July 1847 there was a parliamentary general election and William Dixon Jnr. stood as a Liberal Free Trade candidate for Glasgow. Newspaper reports of his hustings meetings at various locations in the city gave interesting detail with respect to the local issues of the day. At one meeting a question was asked in regard to when the rails were to be uplifted from West Street. Their presence in the street had been an issue with local businessmen and residents,

Rutherglen station was opened in 1849 after the Clydesdale Junction Railway had been established. It grew over the ensuing decades and once boasted nine different platforms with twelve faces, no less. In mid-March 1961, 2-6-4T 42244 has a local bound for the Lanarkshire town of Strathaven. Photograph W.A.C. Smith.

You'll Remember those Black and White Days...

even before he sold the line to the Caledonian.

Dixon neatly side-stepped any involvement in the matter by pointing out that it was the problem of one of his rival candidates in the election. He declared that the questioner should have taken his query to Alexander Hastie, who was a merchant and one of the old money Liberals and the Lord Provost of Glasgow. With particular malice he made great play of the fact that Hastie was also the chairman and leading shareholder of the Caledonian Railway Company who were by then responsible for the old Polloc and Govan Railway's track route and such properties as a redundant engine shed located on West Street, close to the Glasgow, Paisley and Ardrossan canal.

In July 1847, doubtless connected with the election and possibly even encouraged by William Dixon Jnr., legal opinion was sought by the City's councillors with regard to the encroachment onto city streets by railways. Legal advisors referred to the conditions of any Act and as to whether the company was adhering to these conditions. Clearly the onus was very much upon the Caledonian Railway and Alexander Hastie to resolve any public disquiet about the route along West Street, and the issue was quickly dropped from the electoral fray, although it was Hastie and not Dixon who made it to Westminster when the votes were cast a few weeks later.

In the years that followed, the stretch of line along West Street fell into disuse, but when it had opened in 1840 it was a valuable forerunner to the dock railways of later decades. Steam engines progressed up and down the street, separated from the public by iron fences located on either side of the tracks at 25 feet apart. In plans of the early 1830s it was projected that steam locomotives would haul coal laden wagons to a complex of tracks and turntables at Dixon's coal berth. Wagons would be unhitched and run down to the harbour's edge where a tipping mechanism tilted the body of the wagon and enabled the coal to pour into the collier ship berthed alongside. The locomotives then returned to the various collieries with the empty trucks for re-loading.

Three steam locomotives owned by the Polloc and Govan Railway eventually found their way onto the tracks of the Wishaw and Coltness Railway for use on the company's Cleland and Omoa branches. Ironically, under the later ownership of the Caledonian Railway, and numbered 83, 84 and 85, they were purchased back by William Dixon Jnr., for use on and between his collieries and ironworks at Govanhill in Glasgow and at Calder in Coatbridge, Lanarkshire. As part of the deal in selling the Polloc and Govan and Clydesdale Junction Railways to the Caledonian, the Dixon companies were given running powers over the

tracks of the main railway companies. This arrangement existed until as late as 1937.

Locomotive No.83 was acquired in 1854, and Nos.84 and 85 in 1852, when they were altered to 0-4-0 saddle tanks. Between 1855 and 1858 Dixon hired Caledonian Railway 0-4-2 No.95 *Hercules*. Built by R.&W. Hawthorn in 1844/45, it had 14ins. x 20 ins. cylinders and 4ft. 6in. and 2ft. 11 in. diameter wheels. Dixon eventually purchased the locomotive outright in 1858 and had it renamed *Calder No. 5*. Thereafter it was used for hauling coke traffic between Calder, Blantyre and Govan.

The colour of Dixon's engines has yet to be identified, but under the ownership of the Wishaw and Coltness they would have been of a light green livery, and under the Caledonian they would have been of that company's celebrated blue livery.

It was not until 1867 that the lines were uplifted from West Street. By then the Polloc and Govan Railway's route miles had existed for little more than a quarter of a century. One early twentieth century Glasgow historian had claimed that the West Street stretch was little more than a glorified tramway, and as such it predated Glasgow's later passenger tramway system by a few decades.

In early June 1954, Caley 'Jumbo' 0-6-0 57419 starts out from Glasgow Central with an evening service to Strathaven. Much of the former Polloc & Govan and Clydesdale Junction route evolved into such suburban lines, to many coal mining and iron producing Lanarkshire towns, including Coatbridge, Motherwell, Airdrie and Shotts. Photograph W.A.C. Smith.

You'll Remember those Black and White Days...

Sixties Seasons at Temple Meads

Passengers in the fashions so redolent of the period crowd forward (top) to join the 2.15pm to Paddington, under that lovely sweeping roof at Bristol Temple Meads on 28 April 1962. The Warship is the last of the Swindon series, D870 ZULU introduced late the previous year. To judge from the passengers' clothing April 1962 was far from being a balmy one but a few months before, on New Years Eve 1961, Bristol was in the grip of something far worse – witness D811 DARING in bitter conditions. The relaxed crew must have been glad they didn't need that iced-up water column... Photographs Peter Barnfield.

You'll Remember those Black and White Days...

Freight trains on Southern lines were not so obvious. There were certain prohibited hours for a start for the operation of goods trains in the London area, especially transfer traffic from the northern and western lines, to give priority to passenger commuter traffic. So they had to be winkled out by the enthusiast, such as in this instance from a bygone age. Ashford (Kent) was a market town and had a large cattle market served by rail. 31878 passes by eight or more cattle trucks as it runs in off the Maidstone East line with a mixed freight which doubtless originates at Hither Green. 31878 was one of the three-cylinder 2-6-0 N1s built in 1930 for freight work, totalling no more than six locomotives. They all survived until November 1962 when no further work could be found for them. BRILL Vol.10 No.8 (May 2001) has an article giving the history of the class.

The traveller could hardly fail to notice long coal, coke or iron ore trains in other parts of the country but in the south such trains had to be sought out.

You'll Remember those Black and White Days...

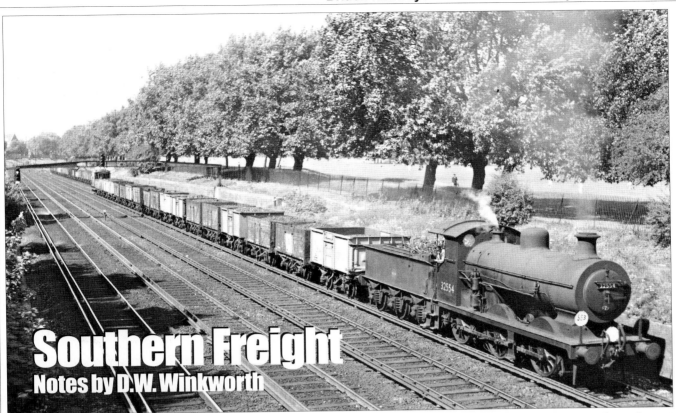

Southern Freight
Notes by D.W. Winkworth

There was a small (compared with other parts of the country) coal producing area in East Kent with outlets at Betteshanger, Chislet, Snowdown and Tilmanstone but most of the output was used locally and warranted no lengthy trains to other parts of the Southern. There was, however, a traffic in coal into London from other parts of the country for which a ring of 'foreign' coal depots was established round the south of the capital (see BRILL, Vol.12 No.1 October 2002 for details of these). This is a train of domestic coal forming the 2.15pm service from Lillee Bridge to Peckham Rye (due 3.46pm) passing Wandsworth Common in charge of C2X 0-6-0 32554.

There was some specialised traffic worked by ordinary freight trains such as in 'Presflo' wagons seen here with K class 2-6-0 32351. The location has not been identified but one BRILL irregular suggests it could be the 3.45pm freight from Beeding Cement Works to Hove but others have doubts ('A Reader Writes' awaits a knowledgeable solution). Southern Moguls of various sorts would appear on freight duties at points as far apart as Bodmin and Dover; this example is of LBSCR origin. The LSW preferred 4-6-0s to 2-6-0s while the SEC had a dozen or so 2-6-0s, added to in SR days as the N class. Photographs E. Trotter, S. Creer and Lucas Collection, The Transport Treasury.

You'll Remember those Black and White Days...

Boston — Hub of East Linc

By Bryan Wilson

By 1842, Boston was sending three vessels a week to London and one each to Hull and Newcastle. Shipping traffic, including passengers, also passed along the River Witham to Lincoln. While it was 1884 before a 'proper' dock was completed, the railway, in the shape of the East Lincolnshire line, arrived on 2 October 1848. The 'Loop' line of the great Northern Railway arrived from Lincoln fifteen days later and was the first part of the GNR to open to the public.

1. The Shed

The first known engine shed was a 'temporary' affair early in 1849, near what was also the 'temporary' station. The permanent shed on the Spalding side of the station, south of Broadfield Lane, was complete by mid-1851. It had nine roads with three gables each covering three roads under slated roofs.

Workshop facilities were provided by the short-lived GNR 'Works'. Following the removal of all major work to Doncaster in 1853, the

erecting shop was reduced from three to two roads to give more room to work while the smithy and turnery were bricked up. This surviving erecting shop found use many years later, in preference to the existing steam shed, when the first diesel shunters came.

In 1852 a 40ft turntable was provided. This was renewed in 1868 on its existing pit but something better was required by the turn of the century and, in 1900, a 54ft version was placed directly outside

When new L1 2-6-4 tanks arrived at Neasden in the late 1940s the GC A5s were put out to fresh pastures. 69815 had ten days 'on trial' at Boston in January 1949 which resulted in 69809, 69810 and 69824 arriving later in the month. They soon made themselves at home on the Skegness and Horncastle branches and examples were present at Boston until March 1959 when the last, 69808, left for Lincoln. This is the latter in good shape 'on shed' on 23 June 1958. The box in the background is Sleaford Junction. The wheel eventually turned full circle when, at the end of 1962, Boston sent Ivatt 4MTs to Colwick to see off the L1s there! Photograph R.C. Riley, The Transport Treasury.

hire

R&M Engineer, within the Lincoln Running & Maintenance Area. Naturally, he was still called 'Shedmaster'.

2. The Works

The Great Northern decided in February 1848 to locate locomotive and rolling stock workshops at Boston 'as a temporary arrangement'. The decision had been made to build the 'Loop' from Peterborough to Lincoln first to earn some money but at the time it had not been decided where the permanent works should be located. Boston was of course convenient as materials could be brought in by sea, both for local use and for the wider railway. Work started by the end of 1848 but the facilities were not completed until several months after the 'Loop' line opened throughout for traffic. In June 1851 Doncaster (from a short list which included both Huntingdon and Grantham) was selected for the main works, on the basis that it was 'better situated for obtaining a supply of labour, coal and iron'.

Doncaster was firmly established by March 1853 and most of the Boston workforce transferred there. Depending on what you read (or believe) it looks as if 300 men and their families moved to Yorkshire. The 'temporary' buildings, at the north (Broadfield Lane) end of the site, then served as the repair shop for Boston engine shed.

the former Works smithy. A brick-built coaling shed was provided by the late 1880s using half ton bucket cranes. This sufficed until a 100 ton capacity mechanical coaler was provided in 1935. In 1955, the shed was modestly improved when the side walls were refurbished and the rear wall reconstructed. The rebuilt roof had an all steel frame but retained the three gables. The old 1850s columns still supported it. From some angles this produced a 'hotchpotch' look but it looked more

modern and sufficed until closure came on 5 January 1964.

Boston originally had a 'Foreman in Charge', Sacre being the first. This post became District Locomotive Superintendent from 1858 and this position had not changed by 1900. In 1918, Boston was part of the Peterborough District which also included the sub sheds at Spilsby and Wainfleet. Again a foreman was in charge. From about 1958 Boston was a 'Running and Maintenance' (R&M) Depot under an

3. The Dock

Boston Dock had its own railway system connected to the Great Northern by a swing bridge across the Haven. After the Sutton Bridge debacle, when the Dock collapsed soon after opening, the GN decided not to contribute to the cost of Boston Dock and only slowly spent money on alterations to their sidings to connect with the Dock lines. The gatehouse, with a 12 lever ground frame, was provided by Boston Corporation and taken over by the

This is the area of Boston shed and station early in the last century, before the Great War. Some of the various subjects of the article have been noted by a letter reference. Crown Copyright Reserved.

Station

Station Hotel

Allan House

G.N.R. Workshops

Schools

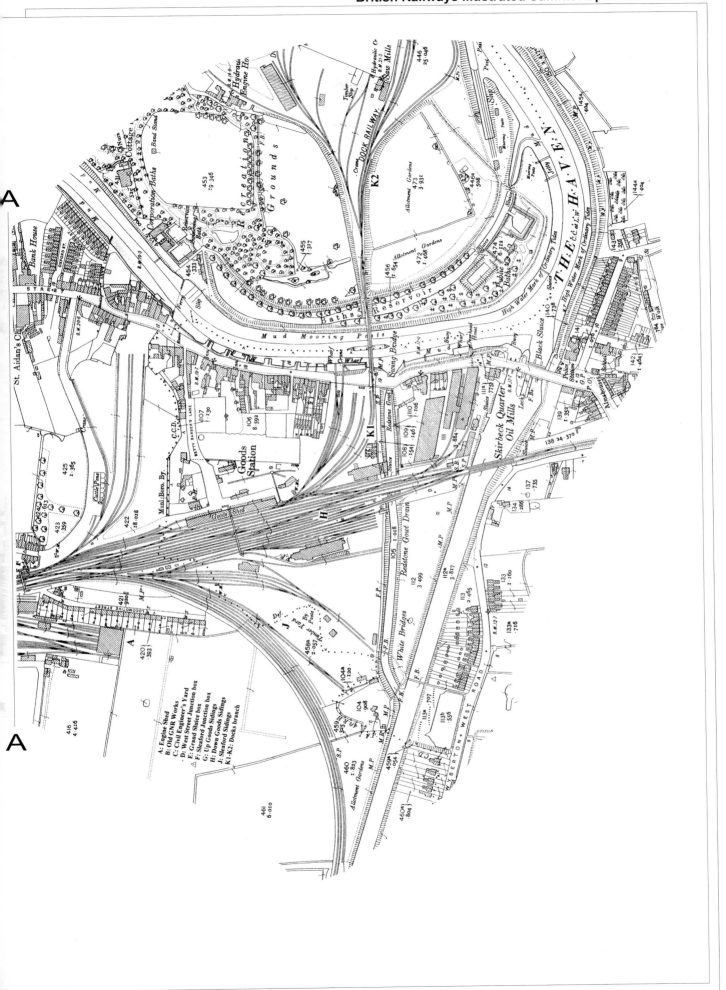

A: Engine Shed
B: Old GNR Works
C: Civil Engineer's Yard
D: West Street Junction box
E: Grand Sluice Junction box
F: Sleaford Junction box
G: Up Goods Sidings
H: Down Goods Sidings
J: Sleaford Sidings
K1-K2: Docks branch

GNR in 1892. It was 31 January 1885 when a GNR engine first moved trucks onto the Dock Quays, but relations improved and a sack store and further sidings were provided. Coal exports and timber imports developed plus some fish traffic. In 1909, the total trade through the port was 750,000 tons. Until 1930, the railway carried the bulk of inland shipments. Boston was the GNR's chief revenue earning station in Lincolnshire. In more recent years, steel has been dealt with, together with roadstone from Mountsorrel in Leicestershire.

Originally the Dock traffic was worked by GNR J54/55 0-6-0Ts. These were displaced by ex-Great Eastern J68s and J69s at the end of the 1920s. 'Diesel Dawn' came in 1956 in the shape of Class 05s. In 1949, the Dock traffic justified a 14 hours a day pilot loco plus another on 'transfer' work, 'as required by the Goods Agent'.

4. Hall Hills Sleeper Depot

A Mr Bethell started a creosote works in Boston in 1851. In 1887 the GNR purchased this establishment, possibly to calm Boston Corporation

who, after 34 years, were still aggrieved at the loss of work to Doncaster and had made a further deputation for an increase in railway work in the town. The site of the plant, to the south of the engine shed towards the South Forty Foot Drain, was deemed inadequate and in 1900 the GNR purchased 28 acres of land at Hall Hills, north-west of the town adjacent to the Lincoln line for a major sleeper depot. Hall Hills signal box, which controlled entry to the site, opened on 10 February 1902. The new depot opened two years later.

The first recorded 'regular' locomotive at the site was GNR 0-6-0T No.470A, (then 3470A) an 1872 rebuild of an 1863 Manning Wardle saddle tank. It became an 0-4-2T in 1914 by the simple expedient of removing the rear portion of the coupling rods and from then on was oil fired. It came to Hall Hills in December 1921 and remained until withdrawn in April 1927. Its replacement was Y1 Sentinel shunter No.4801 (it became 4991 in September 1937). In February 1940 it was superseded by Y3 No.49 which in varying subsequent guises – 8166,

68166 then Departmental No.7 – stayed until July 1961. While the allocation of both the Y1 and Y3 was 'long term', there were many substitutes over the years viz:- Nos.18, 42, 62, 87, 98 and 172 (pre-1946 numbers) and 8162, 8171, 8179 and 8185 are all known to have worked at Hall Hills, some albeit for short periods and some more than once.

Hall Hills Depot boasted its own engine shed, attached as an appendage to one side of the main building. It looked like a later 'add on'. It is not known when it went out of use but it was not used in BR days and the Departmental was then either stabled in the open or it travelled to the main shed. Hall Hills was significant enough to have its own 'Workmen's' service from Boston station in the morning, returning at teatime. It also qualified for its own train of imported sleepers which ran at 4.0am from Immingham via Grimsby and Firsby, then reversed at Woodhall Junction.

The depot, which closed in spring 1964, also boasted a 2ft 3in narrow gauge system for moving sleeper

Left. K2 61759 on the breakdown train (which included an antique 8-ton hand crane). This was a Westinghouse air brake fitted loco – note the extra pipe on front buffer beam – which worked on the GE Section from 1928 until 1952. It was displaced from Boston by the M&GN closure when many LMS type 4MTs were thrown spare. Photograph R.C. Riley, The Transport Treasury.

Below. Boston will always be remembered for its stud of K2 2-6-0s and, particularly, their work on the Skegness and Mablethorpe summer Saturday trains. A 'vacuum only' engine, 61750 spent 9½ years at Boston; the coaling plant is at left and the Carriage & Wagon Repair Shops to the right on 23 June 1958. J69 tank 68602 is the loco behind. Photograph R.C. Riley, The Transport Treasury.

lengths internally. A suitable Baguley/McEwan Pratt loco was purchased by the GNR for in 1921 and a Ruston diesel of 1940 vintage followed, these being two of the total of only ten narrow gauge locomotives operated by the L&NER. Hall Hills Signal Box closed on 10 January 1965.

5. The Locomotives

In early days, GNR 0-4-2s, 2-4-0s and 0-6-0s ruled the roost. From 1898, various types of 4-4-0s covered the local passenger work with D1s, D2s and D3s all present. Indeed 27 different D2s and 17 different D3s were allocated at Boston in the years following the Grouping.

Local freight settled with the J6 0-6-0s; these covered the 'pick ups' which in many cases called everywhere and perhaps took two sets of men to get to Louth and back. These versatile engines were, however, equally at home on 'all stations' passengers and Saturday expresses to and from Skegness. They carried out this work well into the 1950s. As late as the summer of 1956, the 9.39am passenger from Boston to Peterborough could boast a lively run behind one of these. J2s J3s and J4s were also about and in 1951 a J2 0-6-0 could still be found on a Nottingham-Mablethorpe job.

Other 0-6-0s allocated included GER J17s in the late 1930s, NER J21s in the early years of World War Two and J39s throughout the War, particularly on the 'Doncaster Goods'. There was a brief flirtation with the latter class again in 1958-60.

The Great Northern 'Ragtimers', the K2 2-6-0s, will forever be associated with Boston and particularly the 'Skeggies'. Together with Colwick, they covered a large part of the summer Saturday work until more B1s and K3s were available. Rough they might be for the crews but they did the job. A solitary K3 spent a couple of years at the shed for the afternoon Peterborough parcels. These were followed by redundant 4MT 2-6-0s from the M&GN which saw out steam at the shed.

You'll Remember those Black and White Days...

DEPARTURES FROM BOSTON FOR WHICH BOSTON SHED WAS RESPONSIBLE
(SUMMER WORKING TIMETABLE 1949)
Passenger (Starting times of the turn which included other trains as the day progressed)

6.25am	to Horncastle
7.54am	to Lincoln
9.20am (SX)	to Peterborough North
11.10am	to Grantham
11.25am (FSO)	to Lincoln

On Saturdays there were additional turns from Skegness

Freight
4.55am 'A' Goods to Skegness
6.05am 'B' Goods to Skegness
7.15am LE to Firsby for 8.45 Firsby-Spilsby Goods etc
8.00am 'B' Goods to Grimsby
9.30am LE to Sleaford for 10.20 Gds Sleaford – Ancaster
Engine & Brake to Honington then 11.55 Goods Honington to Boston (arr 6/29pm)
11.45am Engine & Van to Alford Town for 1/40pm Alford Town – Boston Goods (due 8/15pm)
11.45am SX LE coupled as far as Firsby) to the Alford E&V for the 2/30pm Goods Skegness-Colwick (due 9/10) Re-engined at Boston en route and return 10/50pm Colwick-Boston
12/25pm 'B' Goods to Louth
1/20pm 'D' Goods to Lincoln West Yard (due 7/21pm)
1/20pm SO LE to Kirton for Pilot duties until 5/50pm
1/30pm SX LE to Woodhall Junction for 5/20pm 'A' Goods to Boston
3/10pm SX LE to Old Leake for 4/25pm 'A' Goods Old Leake to Ferme Park (Re engined for departure from Boston 8/35pm)
3/20pm 'A' Goods to Sleaford. Used to change over Sleaford outstabled loco which returned with 9/14pm ex Sleaford
3/30pm SX LE to Kirton for Pilot and return 8/20pm Gds to Boston
3/32pm SX LE to Sibsey for 4/45pm 'A' Gds to Ferme Park
4/17pm SX Engine & Brake to Hall Hills. Return with 4/40 Gds to Boston (Sleeper supplies for the GN)
4/30pm SX 'A' Goods to Ferme Park
6/50pm SX LE to Sleaford for 8/15pm 'A' Gds to Colwick and 12.05am Gds Colwick-Boston
8/30pm SO 'B' Goods to New England
8/40pm 'A' Gds Boston-Colwick returned 3.35am Colwick-Boston
9/00pm SX 'EF 3' Gds to Doncaster Decoy
9/45pm SO 'B' Gds to Doncaster Decoy
10/30pm SX 'B' Gds to Doncaster Decoy
11/10pm SX 'A' Gds to Colwick and 4.05am Colwick-Boston
11/44pm SX 'A' Gds to New England
Ballast trains ran as and when required.
NB Most Ferme Park services listed had Boston power only as far as New England.

There was never much of a 'purely passenger' allocation but what there was brought interest. Atlantics of both C2 (GN) and C4 (GC) varieties came, the latter in their dying days and mostly on local freight work. Atlantic tanks in the shape of C12s worked the Spilsby pick-up or passenger while Great Central A5s and N5s together with Great Eastern N7s all had their turn here at the appropriate time and one must not forget the Sentinel at Hall Hills. Strangely Boston never had B1 4-6-0s of its own but its men spent a lot of sweat on the Cleethorpes-London jobs with them.

Inevitably there were 'oddities' like WR Diesel Railcar No.20 on four day trials between Boston-Sleaford and Grantham in the autumn of 1952. Boston's ultimate victor must remain as 'Royal Scot' 6100 itself, on shed in June 1963 and well cleaned by retired drivers, while en route to Butlins at Skegness.

6. The Men

Passenger workings took Boston men to Lincoln, Grantham, Horncastle, Skegness, Nottingham and Mablethorpe. There were also jobs to Peterborough North with some turns, like the Cleethorpes/ Grimsby and Skegness-London services, through to Kings Cross. One indeed, for a while, gave a return trip with the 1.00am Kings Cross-Newcastle as far as Peterborough with a Pacific. At one time, there was also a Fridays Only turn to London which involved 'lodging' at Kentish Town and returning with the 8.0am Kings Cross-Skegness on Saturdays.

Freight turns took Boston men to Skegness, Spilsby, Grimsby, Immingham, Colwick, Lincoln, Horncastle, Doncaster, Grantham, Whitemoor, March, New England and London Kings Cross.

7. Through the Years

Early in the twentieth century, in 1905, Boston was home to 43 locos which included four outbased at the sub-sheds of Wainfleet and Spilsby. At the end of the First World War, the total was 41, with three outstationed. By Grouping the figure had risen to 62 of which eleven were E1 2-4-0s, 16 were GN 4-4-0s and 10 were J6 0-6-0s. There were eight shunting tanks of the J54/55 variety.

By 1931 five Great Eastern 0-6-0 tanks of classes J68/69 had arrived

Vacuum only 61766 on 23 June 1958, a K2 with a tale to tell. It came from South Lynn on the M&GN in 1952, went to Thornton Junction via Cowlairs Works in January 1953 but was obviously unsuitable – perhaps no side window cab was the problem – and returned to Boston two months later. Again, it was the M&GN closure that caused its displacement in 1959. The concrete block this side of the coaler is the World War Two air raid shelter. Photograph R.C. Riley, The Transport Treasury.

You'll Remember those Black and White Days...

An immaculate 61771, 23 June 1958. This engine had three separate spells at Boston – this picture was taken during the final one. The appropriately named Locomotive Street is in the background from where, every now and then, ladies would descend on the Shedmaster's office and throw their grubby smalls on his table demanding 'What are you going to do about this?' Usually a full and frank discussion ensued but things went on much as usual afterwards – until the next time. The loco's front end looks a bit battered, apparently not worrying Driver Herbert Luff or his 'laid back' mate. Photograph R.C. Riley, The Transport Treasury.

to replace the old GN shunters. In 1936 there were 15 4-4-0s, 19 0-6-0s and a couple of K2 2-6-0s, 4630 and 4639 – the latter just been rebuilt from K1. There were eight shunting tanks and a pair of C12 4-4-2 tanks, giving a total of 46 locos.

At nationalisation, Boston (which now included Sleaford sub shed) boasted 49 locos, made up as under:-

K2 2-6-0: 61725, 61731, 61744, 61755, 61760, 61762
D2 4-4-0: 62154, 62179, 62180, 62181
C4 4-4-2: 62900, 62901, 62919, 62920, 62921, 62922, 62923, 62924, 62925
J3 0-6-0: 64115, 64132, 64137
J6 0-6-0: 64180, 64181, 64190, 64196, 64198, 64201, 64204, 64210, 64229, 64242, 64244, 64247, 64248, 62476
J2 0-6-0: 65016, 65017, 65020
C12 4-4-2T: 67387
J69 0-6-0T: 68528, 68543, 68560, 68581
J68 0-6-0T: 68655, 68657, 68658, 68659
Y3 0-4-0: 68166
Total: 49

During 1948 two more C12s arrived but the C4s, having been sent to Boston in the autumn of 1947 to eke out their last days on menial tasks such as the local 'pick-up' goods, were reduced from nine to six. The following year, four more C4s were condemned, replaced by three N7s, 69712, 69716 and 68717 from Stratford displaced by the Shenfield electrification. This was not a 'first' as 69694 had spent a couple of months here in 1948.

May 1950 saw the N7s return to Stratford, together with 69674 which spent a month here en route from Lincoln to the same place. While at Boston these engines worked

passenger and parcels services to Lincoln, Horncastle and Skegness as well as freights to Louth and Sleaford. The last two C4s went in 1950 as did the last D2s, replaced by five A5 4-6-2Ts and three K2s, plus three N5 0-6-2Ts, of which two remained.

The J6 complement was enhanced in May 1951 when 64214, 64276 and 64277 arrived from Ardsley. The 'West Riding' theme was continued in the following year when 64250 and 64260 arrived from Copley Hill in exchange for 64276 and 64277 – perhaps the worn out ones in West Yorkshire were in need of a level playing field for a while.

THE PILOTS – SUMMER 1949 WTT
No 1 Passenger 3.30am to 4.35am thence LE to Skegness for 6.35am Skegness-Firsby
No 2 Passenger 7.0am to 10.0pm or finish
No 3 Passenger 2/0pm to 4/0pm Sunday
No 4 Passenger 6/30pm to 9/0pm Sunday
'A' Goods 6.0am Monday to 6.0am Sunday Down Road shunting
'B' Goods 9.0am Monday to 3.0am Daily South end shunting
'C' Goods 6.0am Monday to 6.0am Sunday Park Sdgs shunting
'D' Goods 11/0pm Mon-Sat to 6.0am Tues-Sun Transfer Trips
Docks
No 1 6.0am to 8/0pm Dock Shunting
No 2 As shipping required. Transfer Pilot Goods to Dock and vice versa. 'Goods Agent Boston to give suitable notice when required'.

J6 0-6-0s were synonymous with East Lincolnshire and Boston had 25 different ones allocated between Nationalisation and February 1962. This is 64180 of the first batch, dating from 1911, with the boiler set forward. It is standing on the coaling road with Sleaford Junction Up Home signals and Boston Goods South Distant behind, on 23 June 1958. The steps just in view lead to the coaling platform. Photograph R.C. Riley, The Transport Treasury.

During 1951 two of the remaining J3s went for scrap. Things were again stable in 1952 when just two K2s arrived. This became the pattern with two more per year arriving in 1953, 1954 and 1955. Just one J6 left (for New England) during 1952.

1953 was a busier year when apart from 61728 and 61745 arriving, five J69 0-6-0Ts arrived. Four of these were from the GE Section to replace the J68s which had been represented at Boston since 1929. It had taken 24 years to standardise the shunting fleet! Also, on the K2 front, 61766 went to Thornton in Scotland, straight from repair at Cowlairs Works, for a couple of months but was presumably unsuitable for their needs (61755 and 61770 had similarly been sent to Eastfield early in 1951 but had stayed there). 1953 also saw the last J3, 64132, go for scrap together with J2 65016, leaving just two J2s to soldier on into 1954 when 65017 went in January and 65020 in July. This left just eleven J6s to represent the GNR 0-6-0 fleet. 67350, Boston's last C12, left for New England in July 1953. The only other change in 1954 was the arrival of 61742 and 61766 to replace the two J2s.

1955 was notable in that Boston

received a K3 2-6-0 (61943) from March in July (if that makes sense!) for the afternoon Peterborough Parcels job – on which it had been known to work through to London. It stayed until November 1957 when it was replaced, yes, by another K2. The 'passenger' contingent was rescued by an N5 and an A5 with

the introduction of Multiple Units which commenced at the end of March 1955.

'Diesel Dawn' came to Boston in 1956 when Barclay, (later Class 05) 11178 arrived from Lincoln. Two more A5s and a K2 were lost during the year, but 14 of the latter type remained.

LOCOS ALLOCATED TO BOSTON BETWEEN 1 JAN 1948 AND 5 JAN 1964		
LMS Class 4MT 2-6-0:	43058-62/4/5/6/8/80/3/5/91/2/3/5	
	43104/7-11/42/3/4/7/8/54/5/7/8/9	Total 32
K2 2-6-0:	61720/5/8/31/6/9/42-6/8/50/1/5/6/7/9	
	61760-3/5/6/7/70/1/3/8	Total 29
K3 2-6-0:	61943	Total 1
D3 4-4-0:	62132	Total 1
D2 4-4-0:	62154/79/80/1	Total 4
C4 4-4-2:	62900/1/2/9/15/9-25	Total 12
J3 0-6-0:	64115/32/7	Total 3
J6 0-6-0:	64171/2/80/1/90/1/6/8	
	64201/4/7/10/4/29/31/42/4/7/8/50/60/72/6/7/8	Total 25
J39 0-6-0:	64712/6/28/9/41/55/823/87/960	Total 9
J2 0-6-0:	65016/7/20	Total 3
C12 4-4-2T:	67350/77/83/7	Total 4
J94 0-6-0T:	68018/70/7	Total 3
Y3 0-4-0:	68162/6/71/9/85	Total 5
J69 0-6-0T:	68499/501/22/8/43/50/4/7	
	60/9/70/81/602/18	Total 14
J68 0-6-0T:	68655/7/8/9	Total 4
N5 0-6-2T:	69256/61/9/80/4/369	Total 6
N7 0-6-2T:	69674/94/712/6/27	Total 5
A5 4-6-2T:	69803/4/8/9/10/2/6/7/9/21/4	Total 11
03 Dsl:	D2023/4/5/7	Total 4
04 Dsl:	D2235/96/8	Total 3
05 Dsl:	11178/9/81/6. D2403/7	Total 6
08 Dsl:	D3442/89/90 D4086	Total 4
		Grand Total 188

The allocation in 1957 was affected mainly by the transfer of Spalding sub-shed from New England right at the end of the year (29 December) giving Boston eight LM Ivatt 2-6-0s and six more J6s. The diesel shunting fleet increased with the arrival of 11179, 11786 displacing two J69s. In February, 69284, Boston's last N5 departed for Langwith.

To summarise, at the end of 1957, Boston was home to one A5 (69808), fifteen K2s, eight 4MTs, fifteen J6s, five J69 tanks, three diesel shunters and the Hall Hills Y3 sentinel. This gave a total of 48 locos, exactly the same number as nine years earlier, but with the additional responsibility of Spalding.

1958 saw even more K2s arrive, making a highest ever total of seventeen for the shed at the year's end. Three more 4MTs came from New England when it was found that, with the addition of Spalding, more cover was required from the smaller Boston complement of locos compared with New England, where 'something was always available'. At the end of the year, eight J39s surprisingly arrived. Of these, six stayed into 1959 and one into 1960. This was at a time when some of these locos were being put to store on the Eastern Region as surplus but 64741 and 64823 at least did some work, the latter taking the last freight on the Spilsby branch, on 30 November 1958. 64728 was the survivor into 1960, being condemned in February of that year.

The class had seen service at Boston between 1938 and 1945 when 64746 and 64748 (as LNER 2693, 2695) worked the night goods lodging turn to Doncaster and carried out summer passenger work (such as it was during those years). To complete the J39 story, 2987 had 15 months here in 1938-39, 3093, 3094 and 3095 came for three months in the summer of 1941 and 1996 stayed for 13 months in 1944-45.

The Midland and Great Northern closure at the end of February 1959 had considerable effect on Boston. No less than seventeen of the M&GN 4MTs descended on 40F of which ten stayed and the remainder moved on to Lincoln or Colwick. The outcome was that all the K2s (sixteen) except one (61742) departed, either transferred or sent for scrap. Nine of the J6s also left. The last A5 69808 went to Lincoln in March and six of the J39s also departed, for Colwick, Doncaster and Lincoln.

Thus Boston started 1960 with just six steam classes represented by K2, J6, J39, 4MT, J69 and Y3 Sentinel, just 36 locos in all. 1960 was, however, a quiet year. Spalding became a 'Signing On Point' on 7 March 1960 with no noticeable effect on Boston's allocation. Just one more 4MT arrived (from Stratford) during the year plus three more diesel shunters, making a total of nine. Significantly, one was a 'new' loco in the shape of D2296 in September – a long time since Boston could boast that.

At long last, 1961 saw the end of the GN 2-6-0s at Boston when 61742 left to become a stationary boiler at New England, replacing 61763. Two more J6s went during the year leaving just 64191 to soldier on until February 1962. Two more 4MTs came from Colwick making a total of 24. Is this the highest number of these at any BR shed? More unusual, in June and July, instead of more diesels, J94 'Austerity' tanks 68018, 68070 and 68077 arrived from Colwick and Hornsey to replace the last J69s. They stayed for just a year until sufficient diesels (and reducing workload) saw them off.

More notable perhaps was the departure of the Hall Hills' Sentinel 68166 (Departmental No.7 since March 1953). There had been a Sentinel on that job since November 1926 when 4801 arrived. It was replaced in February 1940 by the Y3

This is one of the second batch of J6s, 64190 with the boiler set back further in the frames. Note the steam heating fittings beneath the front buffer beam. These locos were no strangers to passenger work. Photograph R.C. Riley, The Transport Treasury.

You'll Remember those Black and White Days...

No.49 – which became 68166 in the 1946/48 schemes.

Apart from the two Sentinels mentioned, no less than ten others of the class had spent short spells here, two of them no less than four times, as replacements for the regular loco under maintenance or repair. Usual provision was by Immingham but even Wrexham, Ardsley and Gorton were involved over the years.

After June 1962 Boston was left with just 24 4MT 2-6-0s of which eight went to Colwick in December to see off their L1 2-6-4Ts 'en masse'. Another 'new' loco was D4086 which arrived in February 1962.

All was quiet in 1963 until November when, pending Boston's closure, four 4MTs went to Barrow Hill and the following month four more were condemned leaving just 43058, 43068, 43091, 43092, 43093, 43144, 43147 and 43158 until the shed closed to steam on 5 January 1964. It was demolished soon after. The coaling tower went in 1965 and the turntable was removed in 1967. It remained as a 'signing-on' point for the DMU and shunting drivers

and five DMUs stabled nightly at the station. In 1967, the old Erecting Shop, turnery buildings and repair shops were demolished but the smithy lasted another twenty years. The men were eventually transferred to the station, as were the guards who were formerly located at the Goods Depot. They covered the multiple units, some freight and the pilots.

Today, Boston shed site is a housing estate and any loco 'resting' while its train is loaded or unloaded in the Dock sits in a siding opposite West Street signal box.

8. The 'Sub-Sheds'

No mention of Boston would be complete without reference to the sub-sheds for which it was responsible. First on the scene was Horncastle, a single road shed which looks as if it opened with the branch in August 1855. (It was certainly there by September 1857). The normal occupant was one tank engine, supplemented, it seems, by a small tender engine in early years. It had closed by 1918. In the branch's later years, Boston worked the early parcels train to Horncastle

and the first passenger back while the Lincoln goods trip covered passenger work in the middle of the day. A return Boston trip in the evening completed the day's events. There was no turntable or coaling stage, engines taking coal from a wagon at Kirkstead (Woodhall Junction).

Spilsby came into the picture on 1st May 1868 when the branch opened; likewise the little shed accommodated one tank engine. Stirling 0-4-4Ts, followed by C12 4-4-2Ts from 1921, were the staple fare. Passenger services over the branch ceased with the outbreak of World War Two but the shed did not close until 1941 after which, engines were provided direct from Boston.

Wainfleet was a slightly busier shed. It again opened with the branch from Firsby in 1871 and initially because of the lack of a turntable and the requirements of the BOT inspector, housed a 2-2-2 tank engine. With the extension of the line to Skegness, reached by July 1873, and the provision of a turntable at the seaside terminus, tender locos, both 0-4-2s and 2-4-0s appeared, to be replaced by D2

A steam heating specimen, 64247, a long-term Boston resident. No good for out-basing at Spalding this one as no M&GN tablet pick up apparatus is fitted. 23 June 1958. Photograph R.C. Riley, The Transport Treasury.

A J69 0-6-0T which came from Norwich in July 1953 in exchange for a J68, to 'standardise' the tanks at Boston. It remained at 40F until condemned in October 1959. On the tank side, the eagle eye will still see 'L N E R 7195' which it lost in May 1946. A far cry indeed from Great Eastern suburban work. The building behind is the Carriage & Wagon repair shop. Photograph R.C. Riley, The Transport Treasury.

4-4-0s from about 1921. These saw out the life of the shed. Closure came at the end of the 1940s although the men remained at the 'signing on point' until the DMUs came in 1955/56. Wainfleet locos worked to Lincoln, Louth and Mablethorpe as well as on their own branch. The men did not reach Lincoln but did get to Louth via both Alford and Mablethorpe. The shed staff made themselves 'self-contained' with Passed Firemen covering Drivers' vacancies and the replacement fireman coming from Boston. The place was noted for its poor water with a maximum changeover time of three days, and sooner if possible.

Sleaford was 'inherited' from Grantham on 30 September 1930, eight days after the Sleaford-Bourne passenger services ceased. Two locomotives, latterly J6 0-6-0s, covered pilot duties, the Bourne branch freight and any necessary trips on the Cranwell Aviation College branch. They also assisted any 'lame ducks' on through services. Locos were changed over with 'HQ' on the 3.20pm freight from Boston and 9.14pm return. In 1949, the Pilot was continuous between 6.0am Monday and 4.0am Sunday. From 6 October 1958 a diesel shunter took over the remaining duties on two shifts and steam ceased to use the shed. When Boston closed in January 1964, Sleaford again moved its allegiance, this time, strangely, to Colwick. Sleaford goods yard ceased work in

May of the same year and the shed closed. The men transferred to Boston and travelled daily for generally non-existent work. It took the accountants six months to catch up with events and the men were made redundant in November.

Spalding was transferred from New England's responsibility on 29 December 1957. The two road shed dated from 1866 with the opening of the 'Midland & Eastern' to Bourne. A turntable was provided north of the shed near the station. The majority of its work was on the M&GN side with services to South Lynn, Bourne, Holbeach and so on. In previous years there had been work up and down the GN/GE Joint as well – plus of course, four local pilots. About fifteen locos made up the usual complement, latterly LM 4MTs and J6s. Tank engines were in the minority, but here was a place where LMS 4Fs could rub shoulders with GN K2s or something more exotic that had failed on the main line. Following the loss of work with the M&GN closure, Spalding suffered badly in terms of men's seniority and drivers of 60 years of age became firemen again. A 'Signing On Point' was established in place of the shed on 7 March 1960, initially in the former Waiting Room on Platform 7, later in refurbished rooms on the Up Main Platform (No.2). Such diesel shunters as remained were stabled in the yards.

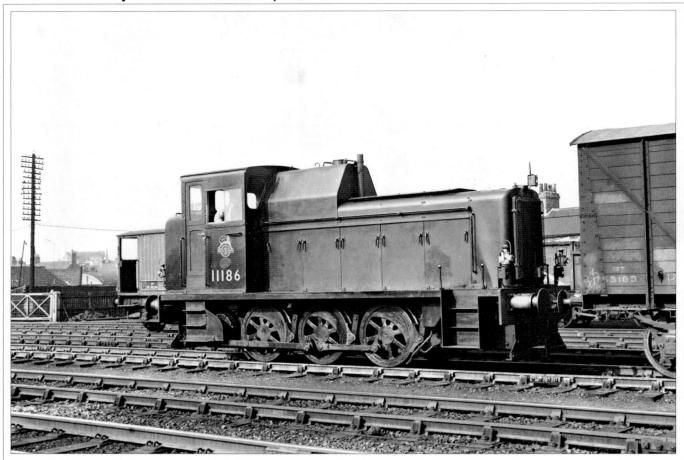

Top left. And this is its replacement, 'Diesel Dawn' in the shape of Barclay-built 11186. It stands near Broadfield Lane level crossing on the Down Goods Line waiting to shunt back towards Sleaford Junction on 23 June 1958. It was part of Class 05 but no '05' number was ever carried on a Barclay loco. It became D2409 in January 1961 but only had twelve years of working life. Photograph R.C. Riley, The Transport Treasury.

Above. Boston power in action. Ivatt 4MT 43060 came to Boston in May 1958 to supplement the Spalding outstation fleet. With an up Class 'F', it stands clear of Broadfield Lane crossing as per instructions. The engine carries an M&GN tablet catcher but stayed only until August 1959 when it passed on to Colwick. The signal is West Street's Down Goods Home. Note the amount of tracks crossing Broadfield Lane at this point – just imagine the 'hassle' they must have caused over the years. Photograph R.C. Riley, The Transport Treasury.

Left. Boston men worked the Immingham B1s to London for some years. Here is 61082 (it spent nearly all its life at Immingham) heading south on an up local on 23 June 1958. Some interesting Departmental vehicles are attached to the ballast trains in the Down sidings. On the left there is a single lever ground frame giving access to these sidings. The single somersault signal (left) protects the exit from the Engine Line and next to it is West Street's Down Main Home with its lower repeating arm. And over on the Up side, that notice reads 'No box wagon to be placed in this siding'. And what is beyond it? A box wagon. Photograph R.C. Riley, The Transport Treasury.

The 'original' K3 2-6-0, 61800 off Immingham with a short up Class 'E' goods. West Street Box is behind the brake van. While the loco will not be overstretched with this load, it already has 38 years to its credit. 61800 then progresses towards Sleaford Junction Box which dates from 1875 when the lines south of Boston station were quadrupled, although the frame is an 1897 replacement. This was an area where shunters used loud hailers to pass messages to the box and the yard pilots used a whistle code, all making life noisy if meaningful. The footbridge led to Locomotive Street but the level crossing only to a dead end – perhaps as well at this busy location. And what detail for modellers – those signal box ornamental bargeboards, the shunters' huts through the bridge and the tender detail on the K3. The box itself closed on 19 May 1974. Photograph R.C. Riley, The Transport Treasury.

Just to show how congested it could get 'on shed'. In March 1958 K3 61866 of Immingham plus local K2 61731 and an unidentifiable J6 lead the field in the sidings between the old Repair Shed (left) and Erecting Shop (right). And what an antique (1881) crane in the breakdown train. Photograph J. Davenport, Initial Photographics.

And finally, a quick look at one of the 'sub sheds', the 1866 Midland & Eastern shed at Spalding. From left to right we have J69 68570, K2 61759, LM 4F 44030 from Nottingham (unusual in that Nottingham engines usually only came as far as Bourne except on their Summer Saturday trips to South Lynn) followed by two more K2s. The lines in the foreground are the M&GN route to Bourne. Photograph J. Davenport, Initial Photographics.

You'll Remember those Black and White Days...

Endpiece

A Southern Region weedkilling train disappears into the Surrey/Sussex hinterland... We hope you enjoyed your 'Summer Special'.

You'll Remember those Black and White Days...